A SCI
INVEST
OF THE OLD TESTAMENT

A SCIENTIFIC INVESTIGATION OF THE OLD TESTAMENT

By

ROBERT DICK WILSON

Ph.D., D.D.,

Late Professor of Semitic Philology in Princeton Theological Seminary

With Revisions By

EDWARD J. YOUNG, Ph.D.

Professor of Old Testament in Westminster Theological Seminary

SOLID GROUND CHRISTIAN BOOKS
BIRMINGHAM, ALABAMA USA

Solid Ground Christian Books
715 Oak Grove Road
Birmingham, AL 35209
205-443-0311
sgcb@charter.net
http://solid-ground-books.com

THE SCIENTIFIC INVESTIGATION OF THE OLD TESTAMENT

Robert Dick Wilson (1856-1930)
Edward J. Young (1907-1968)

Taken from 1959 edition by Moody Press, Chicago, IL
Used with special permission from Moody Press

Solid Ground Classic Reprints

First printing of new edition February 2007

Cover work by Borgo Design, Tuscaloosa, AL
Contact them at borgogirl@bellsouth.net

ISBN: 1-59925-105-1

PUBLISHER'S PREFACE

EVER SINCE FIRST PUBLISHED, *A Scientific Investigation of the Old Testament* has been a benefit to conservative students of the Old Testament. It has provided for them a scholarly answer to many of the scholarly attacks on the Old Testament. For several years, however, the work has been out of print and almost unobtainable even in second-hand bookstores. Moreover, continued discoveries in the Near East have caused it to be somewhat out of date.

Moody Press wishes to express appreciation to Harper and Brothers for permission to reprint this work. The Press is grateful, too, to Dr. Edward J. Young, Professor of Old Testament, Westminster Theological Seminary, for his revisions.

Desiring to leave Dr. Wilson's work intact for the present reader, Dr. Young has brought the subject matter up to date by means of an introductory chapter, footnotes, and appendixes. Usually the reviser's footnotes are followed by an *a*. He has also added extensively to existing footnotes. The reader will be impressed with the fact that practically none of Dr. Wilson's conclusions has been changed. Most of the new information has served to strengthen conclusions which were reached by the author. New discoveries further substantiate and establish the veracity of the Old Testament.

AUTHOR'S PREFACE

IT IS THE PURPOSE of the present volume to show that intelligent Christians have a reasonable ground for concluding that the text of the Old Testament which we have is substantially correct, and that, in its true and obvious meaning, it has a right to be considered a part of the "infallible rule of faith and practice" that we have in the Holy Scriptures.

I have not gone into a discussion of miracles and prophecy, either as to their possibility or as to their actuality. All believers in the incarnation and the resurrection must accept this possibility and this actuality. I seek rather to show that, so far as anyone *knows*, the Old Testament can be and is just what the authors claimed it to be, and what the Christ and the New Testament writers thought it to be. The theory of *kenosis,* so far as it affects the Lord's knowledge of the Old Testament, is, I hope, shown to be unnecessary, because the facts and the evidence bearing upon the Old Testament support the testimony of Jesus.

I have not said much about the chronology and the geography of the Old Testament, because in neither of these two departments of history are the facts and the evidence sufficiently well established to give us reliable testimony upon the details of the Biblical records as they bear upon these two important subjects.

As to the first chapters of Genesis, the extra-Biblical sources now known show that before the time of Abraham the minds of men were much occupied with the origin of the universe; and also, that the account in Genesis is the only one which is clearly monotheistic, and that it is incomparably superior in rationality to the ten or more accounts from Egypt and Babylonia. The Babylonian account of the flood confirms the probability that the Biblical records describe a real historical occurrence, and, as Professor Sayce said long ago, shows by its similar combination of the so-called J and P documents of the Pentateuch that the radical hypothesis of the postcaptivity composition of the Biblical record of the Deluge is absolutely contrary to the facts. The time, the extent, and many of the circumstances of the Flood are still debatable; but that there was a flood before the time of Abraham and that the Genesis account of it is correct is abundantly supported in substance by the evidence of the eleventh tablet of the Babylonian record.

The method followed may be called the evidential method; because I have sought to follow the Laws of Evidence as applied to documents admitted in our courts of law. I presume that the prima-facie evidence of the documents of the Old Testament is to be received as true until it shall have been proved false. I hold, further, that the evidence of manuscripts and versions and of the Egyptian, Babylonian, and other documents outside the Bible confirms the prima-facie evidence of the Biblical documents in general both as to text and meaning; and that this text and meaning cannot be corrected or changed simply in order to be brought into harmony with the opinions of men of our generation. To demand that we should verify every statement of any ancient document (or modern for that matter) before we can reasonably believe it, is demanding the impossible. The most that we can reasonably require is that the author of the document and the document itself shall stand the test of veracity wherever their statements can be examined in the light of other testimony of the same age and provenance and of equal veracity. Examined in this way, I contend that our text of the Old Testament is presumptively correct, that its meaning is on the whole clear and trustworthy, and that we can as theists and Christians conscientiously and reasonably believe that the Old Testament as we have it is what it purports to be and what Christ and the apostles thought it to be, and what all churches have always declared it to be — the Word of God and the infallible rule of faith and practice.

In the title I use the phrase *Scientific Investigation*, because I am trying to judge the Old Testament documents in the light of the facts made known in the documents of the nations who surrounded and influenced the people of Israel through all its history from Abraham to Ezra. Again, I have ventured to use the term *scientific,* not merely because these conclusions are based on knowledge, but because, after the introductory pages, I have presented the evidence in an orderly manner, treating of text, grammar, vocabulary, and history in what I consider to be a logical sequence. The results of some of my investigations, such as those of the foreign words in the Hebrew of the Old Testament, and of the religion of Israel, have not yet been fully published. If it please the Lord to spare my life and grant me health I hope in the future to publish the results of my labors on these and other subjects.

It may help the less learned of my readers if I explain

why I have given so much space to the discussion of text, grammar, and vocabulary.

As to the text, or written form, of the documents of the Old Testament, as they issued from their authors, it is obvious that, if we do not have exact copies of the original writings, it will be impossible for us to be sure that we have the very words of the prophets who wrote or approved these writings. In my discussion of the text, therefore, it is my endeavor to show from the evidence of manuscripts, versions, and the inscriptions, that we are scientifically certain that we have substantially the same text that was in the possession of Christ and the apostles and, so far as anybody knows, the same as that written by the original composers of the Old Testament documents.

As to grammar, since the critics date the documents of the Old Testament largely by the forms and syntactical constructions of the language, it is necessary to show that these forms and constructions are irrelevant as evidence of the time at which a document was written.

As to vocabulary, since all the commentaries and introductions to the Old Testament in general, or to particular books or documents of the Old Testament, are full of conclusions based upon the origin, or meaning of the Hebrew words, both as to the time, place, authorship, and meaning of these books and documents, it is necessary to investigate the history of the Hebrew language and of the particular words produced in evidence, in order to see whether these words really prove what they are alleged to prove, with regard to the origin and contents of the books and documents.

Perhaps at this point it will be well also to give a statement of the conservative and radical views as to the time of the composition of the books of the Old Testament.

The radicals claim, in general, that the Canon was not completed till about 100 B.C., and in particular:

1. That the first six books, that is, the Pentateuch and Joshua, were composed by at least a dozen redactors out of five or more other books (J, E, D, H, and P), which were written from 900 to 450 B.C.; although, with the exception of Ezra, the authors and redactors of these five books are alike unknown to history, either as to name, time, or provenance. The sources of their information are also unknown to history, and consequently no one can rely upon the veracity of any statement in the Hexateuch. The books of Moses are simply a mythical and confused account of the origin of the people and institutions of Israel.

2. That the Book of Judges is "hardly strictly history," but "probably traditions preserved among the individual tribes"; and that it was put in its present form "by a hand dependent on P," i.e., after 450 B.C. Most of the critics now admit that the larger part of the Books of Samuel and Kings is from original sources written at the time of, or shortly after, the events recorded in them. Ruth and Esther are romances, idylls, or historical novels. Chronicles, Ezra, and Nehemiah have some historical matter; the rest was invented for one purpose or another, mostly to exalt the priestly caste.

3. As to Hosea, Amos, Obadiah, Nahum, Habakkuk, Zephaniah, Haggai, Malachi, Ezekiel, and most of Jeremiah, the conclusions of the radical critics as to authorship and date are not very different from those of the conservatives. Jonah and Joel are placed after the captivity; Micah and Zechariah are divided into three parts and scattered over three or more centuries. Isaiah has a dozen or more authors, scattered over four centuries. In all the books anything looking like a prediction is ruthlessly cut out and attributed

to some unknown redactor of an age at, or after, the event. Daniel, because of its apocalypses, is placed about the middle of the second century B.C.

4. As to the other books, the radical critics are united in declaring that the Lamentations was not written by Jeremiah, nor the Proverbs, Ecclesiastes and the Song of Songs by Solomon. Some parts of Proverbs and all of Ecclesiastes are by many assigned to Persian or Greek times. As to the Psalms, most of the critics now deny that David wrote any of them, and many critics put the Psalms after the captivity and assign many of them to Maccabean times. Job is generally assigned to the sixth century B.C.

On the other hand, the conservative position is, in general, that the Canon of the books of the Old Testament was completed in the fifth century B.C., before the succession of the prophets ceased. As to the particular portions of the Old Testament, their view is:

1. That the Pentateuch as it stands is historical and from the time of Moses; and that Moses was its real author though it may have been revised and edited by later redactors, the additions being just as much inspired and as true as the rest.

2. That Joshua, Judges, Ruth, Samuel, and Kings were composed from original and trustworthy sources; though, in the case at least of Kings, they were not completed till about 575 B.C.

3. That the prophets Hosea, Joel, Amos, Jonah, Micah, and Isaiah were all written about or before 700 B.C.; Obadiah, Nahum, Habakkuk, and Zephaniah before 600 B.C.; Jeremiah, Lamentations, and Ezekiel, between 650 and 550 B.C.; Daniel, Haggai, and Zechariah between 550 and 500 B.C.; and Malachi in the fifth century B.C.

4. That there is good and sufficient reason for concluding

that the headings of the Psalms are as a whole correct; that it is probable that all of the Psalms were written before 400 B.C.; that Ecclesiastes and the Song of Songs and most of the Book of Proverbs may, for all we know, have been written by Solomon; that Esther, Ezra-Nehemiah, and Chronicles were written before 400 B.C.; and Job at 550 B.C., or earlier.

In conclusion, let me reiterate my conviction that no one knows enough to show that the true text of the Old Testament in its true interpretation is not true. The evidence in our possession has convinced me that at "sundry times and in divers manners God spake unto our fathers through the prophets," that the Old Testament in Hebrew "being immediately inspired by God" has "by his singular care and providence been kept pure in all ages"; and that, when the wisdom of men and the law of God had alike failed to save humanity, in the fullness of time, when all the preparation was complete, God sent forth His Son to confound the wisdom of man and to redeem those who come under the Law. Thank God for the Holy Oracles. Thank Him yet more for "the unspeakable gift" of His love, who brought life and immortality to light in His Gospel.

CONTENTS

ABBREVIATIONS FREQUENTLY USED

CT—*Cuneiform Texts from Babylonian Tablets, etc., in the British Museum.*

H,P,J,E,D—See *Hexateuch in Glossary.*

KAT—*Die Keilinschriften und das Alte Testament,* by Eberhard Schrader.

KB—*Die Keilinschriftliche Bibliothek* or Cuneiform Library (contains translations into German of the leading historical, poetical, and contractual inscriptions of the Assyrians and Babylonians).

LOT—*An Introduction to the Literature of the Old Testament,* by S. R. Driver.

LXX—An abbreviation for The Seventy or The Septuagint.

O. T.—Old Testament.

PSBA—*Proceedings of the Society of Biblical Archaeology.*

PTR—*Princeton Theological Review.*

TSBA—*Transactions of the Society of Biblical Archaeology.*

VASD—*Vorderasiatische Schriftdenkmäler.*

ZATW—*Zeitschrift für die Altestamentliche Wissenschaft.*

INTRODUCTION

The life and ministry of Robert Dick Wilson

OCCASIONALLY God gives to His Church a man of unusual gifts, deep piety, and true insight. Such a man was the late Robert Dick Wilson. Dr. Wilson lived at a time when the Old Testament was being subjected to some of the severest attacks and criticisms that it had ever received. He himself was a devout Christian and grieved over these attacks. He also had an insight into their nature and into the need for refuting them. And he had the God-given ability for standing up to the challenge which these attacks constituted, accepting it and seeking to answer.

Wilson was born on February 4, 1856, at Indiana, Pennsylvania. His undergraduate studies were taken at the College of New Jersey which later came to be known as Princeton University. In 1876 he received the degree of bachelor of arts, to be followed in 1879 by the master's and in 1886 by the doctor's degree. At Western Theological Seminary in Pittsburgh, Wilson pursued his theological training, and this was followed by two years in the University of Berlin, Germany, primarily devoted to the study of the Semitic languages.

With this training and preparation, Wilson was ready

to plunge into his lifework, the defense of the Old Testament as the Word of God. Great tasks demand men of great preparation, and those whom God has mightily used in His Church have often been men whose preparation and training have been thorough. The study of Latin and Greek, together with a full course in theology and the later training in Semitics were to serve as a firm foundation for Dr. Wilson's later studies. In addition to these he possessed a thorough knowledge of German, without which it is today impossible to do competent work in the field of Old Testament studies.

It was at Western that Wilson began his labor of teaching, first as instructor and then as professor. In 1900 he was called to Princeton Theological Seminary. There he found himself in the atmosphere of intelligent loyalty to the Bible which had always characterized that seminary. He stood in the line of men such as Joseph Addison Alexander and William Henry Green, and he carried on that line, plunging at once into the earnest and intellectual defense of the Old Testament.

In the year 1902 Friedrich Delitzsch, son of the great Biblical scholar Franz Delitzsch, had delivered a lecture before the Kaiser of Germany in which he had claimed that the Old Testament was greatly influenced by the religion of Babylon. At the opening exercises of Princeton Seminary for 1902, Dr. Wilson was the speaker and he offered a devastating reply to Delitzsch. This lecture was but a beginning; for throughout his life, Wilson continued a sustained defense of the Old Testament Scriptures.

It is of course impossible for one man to consider thoroughly all the questions involved in the study of Scripture, and Dr. Wilson was aware of this. As his particular field of specialty, he chose the Book of Daniel. This was a happy choice, for this book had been under particularly heavy fire. According to Jesus Christ (Matt. 24:15) a certain prophet by the name of Daniel had predicted the abomination of desolation. This particular utterance, however, forms an integral portion of the Book of Daniel, so that if the prophet spoke this prophecy, he must have spoken the remainder also.

The Biblical position, notwithstanding the witness of Christ, by no means found universal acceptance. The Book of Daniel was denied by many to Daniel as its author. Instead, the claim was raised that the book was composed during the second century B.C. It was supposedly written to encourage the Jews in their uprising at the time of the Maccabees. In opposing this non-scriptural view of the origin of the book Wilson exhibited tremendous learning. A series of scholarly articles began to appear, and in 1917 a volume entitled *Studies in Daniel*. To the very end of his life this faithful servant of God wrote in defense of the Book of Daniel.

To think that Dr. Wilson's defense of the faith was confined to the classroom would be to do him an injustice. Unlike many, Wilson had a deep concern for the doctrinal purity of the Church to which he belonged, and which by solemn vow he had promised to defend. The seminary at which he taught had long been noted for its unswerving loyalty to the Bible. Within the Church, however, were modernists and doctrinal indifferentists and others who did not want the seminary to stand uncompromisingly upon the Bible but rather that it represent the entire Church.

These opponents of Princeton's high loyalty to Scripture won their case. What was Dr. Wilson to do? Should he remain at Princeton and simply confine his efforts to teaching in the classroom? There were men who did just that.

Wilson, however, was not one of them. Loyalty to Christ and to His holy Word had first claim upon him. Hence, with J. Gresham Machen, Oswald T. Allis, Cornelius Van Til, and others he was instrumental in founding a new seminary, Westminster, in Philadelphia. Here he continued with unabated zeal until his death on October 11, 1930.

Wilson's pen was ever busy. For the most part his writings were of a technical nature, intended for the specialist in Old Testament studies. There was one pamphlet, however, which was written for the average Christian reader, and which, because of its wide influence and intrinsic merit, should be singled out for mention. This pamphlet bore the name *Is the Higher Criticism Scholarly?* and was translated into Swedish, Portuguese, Dutch, French, Chinese, Korean, and Japanese. In this work Wilson gave expression to his conviction that many of those who were attacking God's Word were not facing the facts. In other words, they were not employing methods that were truly scholarly.

To the very end of his life Dr. Wilson remained true to the Bible as the infallible Word of God. In speaking to his students shortly before his death, Wilson declared, "I have made it an invariable habit never to accept an objection to a statement of the Old Testament without subjecting it to a most thorough investigation, linguistically and factually. If I find that the objector bases his objection upon a general theoretical consideration such as the denial of miracles or of predictive prophecy, I just smile at the objector and turn him over to the department of theism, to learn who and what the God of the Bible is. 'He that sitteth in the heavens shall laugh' at them, and I for one laugh with Him. But if a man believes in the probability or certainty of miraculous events wherein God is working but is precluded from faith in the claims of the Bible to be a divine revelation by doubts based upon alleged historical, scientific, or philological evidence, then I consider it to be my duty to do my best to show that this alleged evidence is irrelevant, inconclusive, and false."[1]

On October 11, 1930, Dr. Wilson was taken to be with the Lord. Two weeks previously at the opening exercises of the seminary, he had spoken a few words of greeting to the new students. Illness came upon him suddenly, and he was taken to the Presbyterian Hospital in Philadelphia. Thus there passed from the scene a great Christian warrior and defender of the faith.

A Scientific Investigation of the Old Testament is a work in which the results of Dr. Wilson's studies are presented. Almost every statement in the book is based upon long and patient research. For this reason the book may be a bit difficult to read. Its reading, however, will be amply rewarding to the man who wishes to understand how strong is that evidence which corroborates the Old Testament.

It will be necessary to say a word as to why this volume does not make easy reading. The Old Testament was written in Hebrew, a language which not only is written and read from right to left (in contradistinction to English) but which is also written in an alphabet of square characters. These characters represent only consonants, the vowels being indicated by little signs which are placed within, below, and above the consonant. In the Hebrew language there are found influences from different sources, with the result that Hebrew may truly be said to be a mixed language. The result is that Hebrew appears to have many exceptions to almost every rule and is a difficult language to learn. It is true that a sight-reading knowledge of Hebrew prose may be obtained in a year or so, but the ability to read the entire Old Testament comes only as a result of long and arduous labor. Dr. Wilson had mastered this difficult language.

---

[1]*Christianity Today*, Vol. 1, No. 2, June, 1930, p. 5.

One who wishes to do thorough work in the Old Testament must know Hebrew — that goes without saying; but he will be greatly aided in his task if he has a competent knowledge of some of the languages and dialects which are cognate to Hebrew. It has been said that Wilson was at home in some forty-five languages and dialects, even including the Armenian. Today the list would increase, for the languages of Ugarit, as well as the Akkadian of Nuzi and Mari must now be taken into account.

Only one who has done similar work himself can appreciate the tremendous amount of toil which the following pages represent. But anyone who will read these pages carefully will soon come to see that the Old Testament is capable of scholarly defense and that Robert Dick Wilson was one of its most scholarly defenders. Because of his painstaking research many have been strengthened in their faith and many ministers have preached with greater earnestness and devotion than would otherwise have been the case. For it is on men such as Wilson, men who have not feared hard work, who have not shirked the difficult problems, and who have been willing to join the battle with the enemy that God has built His Church. May the triune God be praised for having given to His people so great a warrior as Robert Dick Wilson.

I

THE METHOD OF THE INVESTIGATION

IN THE COMMON LAW OF ENGLAND, which is followed in most of our American commonwealths, the presumption is that the accused is innocent of an alleged crime until he shall have been proved guilty. It may be called the evidential system of jurisprudence. In contradistinction to this is the inquisitorial system in which the accused is supposed to be guilty unless he can establish his innocence. These two systems have their followers when we leave the forum of legal combat and enter that of Biblical literature and history. Those who pursue the inquisitorial method accuse the authors of the Old Testament books of anachronisms, inconsistencies, frauds, forgeries, and false statements, and boldly defy anyone to disprove their accusations. The would-be defenders of the authors are very much in the position of a man who would have defended a friend in the clutches of the Spanish inquisition.[1] He could not gain access to the accused and the accused had no means of communicating with him, except through the inquisitors themselves. So Moses and Isaiah and Jonah are unable to communicate with us who would defend them; and those who accuse

---

[1] See Emil Reich, *The Failure of the Higher Criticism of the Bible.*

them, or their works, of misstatements and falsehoods wrest their words, stigmatize their motives, assume that their own opinions are testimony, and declare a verdict of guilty. They denounce as unscientific any attempt on the part of the defenders to establish the truthfulness and harmoniousness of the documents. They set themselves up as accusers, witnesses, jury and judges, and call unscholarly and traditional (word of scorn!) all who refuse to accept their verdict. They cry aloud: To the auto-da-fé with the book and with all the defenders thereof!

EXAMPLES OF CRITICAL METHODS
GENESIS 14

One of the most outstanding examples of the inquisitorial method of criticism is Genesis 14, where we have the account of the expedition of Chedorlaomer against the kings of Sodom and Gomorrah. Of this expedition and of the defeat of it by Abraham, Wellhausen says that they "are simply impossibilities." When it is shown that the kings of Babylonia had made similar expeditions as far as the Mediterranean in the time of Lugal-zaggizi and Sargon the First (cir. 3000 B.C.),[2] and in the time of Hammurabi (2000 B.C.)[3] and that in the time of Hammurabi, there were kings with the names of Arioch, Tidal, and with at least the first part of the name Chedorlaomer,[4] that a man with the name of Abram is mentioned as early as 1950 B.C.,[5] the critics reply that some unknown Jewish archaeologist of some time between 900 and 300 B.C., who happened to be in Babylon, concocted this little story in glorification of Abraham and succeeded in in-

---

[2] King, *A History of Sumer and Akkad*, 197, 360.

[3] Jeremias, *The Old Testament in the Light of the Ancient East*, I, 317, 322.

[4] E. g., Kudur-Maburg, and Kudur-Nahundu. See King, *The Letters and Inscriptions of Hammurabi*, I, LV.

[5] See able discussions of Gen. 14 in Clay, *Light on the Old Testament from Babel*, 125-143; and Pinches, *The Old Testament in the Light of Historical Records of Assyria and Babylonia*, p. 148.

ducing Ezra and Nehemiah, or some later Jewish authorities before 280 B.C. (when the Septuagint translation was made),[6] to accept the fabrication as fact and to embody it among the archives of the Jewish people, by whom it has ever since been considered to be authoritative history.

In favor of the historical character of this narrative we have the evidence that it suits the time and the place, that the names of some of the principal actors are known to be names of persons living in the time of Hammurabi, that the names of the three kings confederated with Chedorlaomer have been identified as kings of the time of Hammurabi, that Elam had at that time and never afterward the hegemony of Western Asia, that expeditions of the kind were common from 4000 B.C. to the time of the Persians and that oriental armies have again and again been put to flight by a sudden attack of inferior forces.[7]

Against the historical character of this narrative we have the assertion of Wellhausen and other critics of our times (only about 4,000 years after the supposed expedition!) that the expedition was *"simply impossible,"* and that it is probable that the account may have been fabricated (or forged) by some person unknown, at some time unknown, in some way unknown, and accepted as true history by some persons unknown, at some time unknown, for reasons unknown. Not one item of evidence in the way of time, place, logic, psychology, language, or customs, has been produced against the truthworthiness of the document. The prima-facie evidence is supported by the circumstantial evidence. But a German professor says it is "simply impossible"; English followers echo "simply impossible," and the Americans echo

---

[6] Or, probably, before 400 B.C., the latest date at which the Samaritans could have acquired their copy of the Pentateuch.

[7] See Reich, *Loc., cit.*, p. 81, Sayce PSBA, 1918, and Pilter PSBA, XXXV. 205-216.

again "simply impossible." And this assertion of simply impossible is called an "assured result of scientific criticism"![8]

[8] The evidence on Gen. 14 will be found in Hommel, *The Ancient Hebrew Tradition*, pp. 146-200; Albert T. Clay, *Light on the Old Testament from Babel*, pp. 125-143; Alfred Jeremias, *The Old Testament in the Light of the Ancient East*, pp. 314-324; Pinches, *The Old Testament, etc.*; King, *The Letters and Inscriptions of Hammurabi*, I, pp. 49 ff., III, 68 ff., 6-11, 237; Schorr, *Urkunden des Alt-babylonischen Zivil-und-Prozesrechts*, pp. 589, 591, 595, 612; Pilter, *Proceedings of the Society of Biblical Archaeology*, for 1913 and 1914; and many discussions by Professor Sayce.

Since Dr. Wilson's day there has been more and more of a tendency to recognize the historical background of Genesis 14. In its detailed nature verse 1 corresponds with the style of the ancient cuneiform chronicles. On the basis of linguistic grounds (see footnote 12, p. 65) the identification of Amraphel with Hammurabi must now be abandoned. Upon the basis of the chronology which the recently discovered (1935) texts from Mari demand, Hammurabi is to be dated about 1728 B.C., which would be considerably later than the time of Abraham.

Ariok is the same name as Arriwuku, also known from Mari. This does not prove that the two are to be identified, but merely that the name itself may have been widely used. The name Chedorlaomer is Elamitic, and means "servant of Lagamar," an Elamite deity. An Elamite king could easily have borne this name. Tidal reminds us of the Hittite name Tudhalia, but it does not follow from this that these events described in Genesis 14 are to be placed in the seventeenth century B.C.

The lack of a name given to the fifth Canaanite king is a mark of genuineness, for a fabricator would not have allowed such an omission to stand. (v. 2).

In the march of the eastern kings to Kadesh, south of the Dead Sea about 100 kilos, we may see an attempt to control the politically important commercial route which ran on to the Red Sea and so to Egypt. The historicity of the narrative is further shown in its mention of the Rephaim, a fact which formerly had been employed as evidence against its historicity. The phrase *mt.rpi* (man of Rephi) has now been found in Ugaritic. The Horites also, once claimed as evidence of the narrative's unhistorical character, are probably to be identified with the Hurrians of the second millennium B.C. who settled in the region of the upper Tigris. In Genesis 14 the word may have become a general designation for the early inhabitants of Palestine.

The numeral 318, used of Abram's "trained men" is a mark of accuracy, for we learn from the Amarna tablets that this was approximately the size of raiding expeditions. The route which Abram followed in pursuing the kings has been rejected as unhistorical, but it is now known that a line of fortresses was found along this route, which would have made it ideal for Abram's purposes. The word translated "trained servants" (*hanikim*) is found in Egyptian texts to designate retainers about a chieftain. All these details make it clear that Genesis 14 can no longer be regarded as unhistorical.

The Law of Holiness

In contradistinction to the inquisitorial method is that which presumes a man to be innocent until he is proved guilty. As applied to documents it proceeds on the presumption that a document is to be presumed to be what it purports to be until it shall be proved that it is not. Thus the presumption is that the so-called Law of Holiness (Lev. 17-26) was the work of Moses, because seventeen times in these chapters it is said that Jehovah spake unto Moses saying what is in the following section, and because the Law begins with the statement: "Jehovah spake unto Moses saying: Speak unto Aaron and unto his sons and unto all the children of Israel, and say unto them: This is the thing which Jehovah hath commanded," and ends with the subscription (26:46): "These are the statutes and ordinances and laws, which Jehovah made between him and the children of Israel in Mount Sinai by Moses." The superscription and the subscription mention the place, subject matter, original speaker, mediators, and persons addressed. The contents of the chapters seem to substantiate the claim of the superscription and subscription.

The issue, then, is clearly drawn. Anyone who successfully assails the veracity of this document must prove either that there is no Jehovah, or that He cannot address or speak to man, or that there was no Moses or Aaron, or that Jehovah did not speak to Moses, or that there were no children of Israel at that time, or that the laws were not given at Sinai. Its veracity cannot be directly assailed by an attack on its language for the document does not say that it was originally written in Hebrew. Nor would it prove its nonexistence to show that it was not mentioned,[9] nor observed for four hundred or a thousand years after it was written; nor even to show that before the time of Ezra its injunctions were broken and the very opposite of them obeyed. Nor would it show that the document as a whole was not from Moses, if it could be demonstrated that certain parts of it were not from him, the critics themselves being witnesses; for they all claim that there are interpolations in Amos and Jeremiah while upholding their genuineness as a whole.[10] Nor would it show that the Law of Holiness was not given by Moses, if it could be proved that he did not write it with his own hand.[11] Nor would it prove that Moses was not the author of

---

[9] The code of Hammurabi is not mentioned in any known document, except in the code itself. Outside of the *Zadokite Fragments,* there is no evidence for the existence of the Zadokite sect, nor for the practice of their laws. Among the Dead Sea discoveries (see Appendix 2c) fragments of the Zadokite documents were found. As a result of this discovery we now know more about the Zadokite sect than was true in Dr. Wilson's day. There seems to be little serious question but that the manuscripts found in the Dead Sea caves were deposited there by members of the same sect as that of which the so-called Zadokite fragments speak. For an introduction to the entire subject the reader should consult H. H. Rowley, *The Zadokite Fragments and the Dead Sea Scrolls,* Oxford, 1952.

[10] Compare the last section of the Gospel of Mark.

[11] The critics reiterate the statement that it is not said in the Pentateuch that *Moses* wrote any of it except the curse on Amalek, the Ten Commandments and certain other portions, as if this were an unanswerable argument against the Mosaic authorship of the Law. Is one to allege, then, that Hammurabi cannot be called the author of the code named after him, unless, forsooth, he inscribed it with his own hand? And yet the monument expressly ascribes itself to Hammurabi in the words of the epilogue (Col. 41:59-67): "In the days that are yet to come, for all future times, may the king who is in the land observe the words of righteousness which I have written upon my monument." Or, is Sennacherib not to be called the author of Cylinder No. 103,000, unless he himself inscribed it? Yet it begins with his name and titles and is full of his words and deeds recorded in the first person, singular number. "I fashioned a memorial tablet," "I set it up," "I flayed Kirua," "I sent my troops." It is all I, I, I, my, my, my, from beginning to end; and yet, it is certain that he never wrote a word of it with his own hand. Or is Darius Hystaspis not the author of the Behistun Inscription, whose sentences are largely in the third person and of which nearly every section begins with "Thus saith Darius the king"? What a subject for the painter's brush! Darius, the Persian Achaemenid,

the Law of Holiness to affirm that the same kind of argument which has been used with regard to it would prove also that Moses was the author of the Law of the Covenant in Exodus 20-24 and of Deuteronomy and of the other documents of the Pentateuch, and that *they* could not have had the same author. For if Jehovah was really the source of all the laws as the documents state, then any apparent inconsistencies between the codes must be possible to harmonize or must be due to errors of transmission, or, at least, will be no more against the consistency of the laws, if they were all written during Moses' lifetime than if they were uttered at widely separated periods of time. And if they were all the production of Moses, and he merely attributed them to Jehovah, this would simply remove the onus of the alleged inconsistencies from the shoulders of Ezra and the later Jews and place it upon the back of Moses. Why must we suppose that Moses would have avoided all inconsistencies, but that Ezra and all the numerous unknown but cunning redactors who are alleged to have composed the Pentateuch should have retained or inserted them? It is passing strange, also, that the Pharisees and Rabbis who tried to observe fully all the laws of the Pentateuch and actually thought they were doing so, should have failed to find in them those inconsistencies which to the modern critic seem so numerous and incomprehensible and irreconcilable.

Nor is there anything in The Law of Holiness that may not have been written 1,500 years before Christ as well as

king of Babylon and of the lands, king of Upper and Lower Egypt, sitting on a scaffolding, his chisel in his left hand and his mallet in his right, cutting into the imperishable rock the record of his achievements by the grace of Ahuramazda! And how about Thothmes I and III, and Ramses II, III and XIII, and Shishak, and Tiglath-Pileser I and III, and Nebuchadnezzar I and II, and others, whose numerous and lengthy records have been preserved? Are we to suppose that Moses cannot have recorded his thoughts and words and deeds just in the same way that his predecessors, contemporaries, and successors, did?

500 years before. Indeed, we can scarcely conceive of a human society so ignorant as not to have understood all of its injunctions. No lawyer is needed to explain its simple, clear, and concise language; and it is concerned with everyday matters, such as the shedding of blood, the relation of the sexes, and duties to parents, strangers, and God.[12]

Nor can it be shown that there are any geographical or archaeological references in the Law of Holiness that are unsuitable to the age of Moses. Nor can it be shown that the ideas of Holiness are such as could not have been known to Moses, or that they are so different from the ideas of JE, D and P as that they could not all have proceeded from the fertile brain of one man and age.[13] Where the ideas of the different documents are the same and are expressed in the same language, they may of course have been by the same author. Where the ideas differ in phraseology but are substantially the same, this is also no indication of different au-

---

[12] The following is an analysis of the Law of Holiness: 16, the day of atonement; 17, laws concerning blood; 18, laws of incest and lust; 19, 20, laws of holy living such as fearing parents (19:3), rejecting idols (v. 4), offering acceptable peace offerings (vv. 5-8), helping the poor (vv. 9, 10), forbidding stealing and lying and profanity (vv. 11, 12), defrauding the workingman (v. 13), injuring the deformed (v. 14), perverting judgment (v. 15), being a talebearer or hater of neighbors (vv. 16, 17), vengeance (v. 18), mingling of cattle, seed, or textiles (v. 19), fornication (vv. 20-22), eating of holy fruit (vv. 23-25), or blood (v. 26), practicing magic (v. 26,) or multilation (vv. 27, 28), or prostitution (v. 29), profaning the Sabbath or the sanctuary (v. 30), defiling themselves with familiar spirits, etc. (v. 31), dishonoring the aged and stranger (v. 32), and falsifying the weights and measures (vv. 35, 36), giving seed to Moloch (20:1-5) wizards (v. 6), cursing parents (v. 9), adultery (vv. 10-21); 21 and 22, laws concerning holiness of priests; 23, the feasts; 24, 25, various laws such as that concerning the oil and the lamp (vv. 1-4), the shewbread (vv. 5-9), blasphemy (vv. 10-16), and the *lex talionis* (vv. 17-22); 26, epilogue.

[13] The reader will understand that the critics divide the first six books of the Bible (called the Hexateuch) into five principal documents; the Deuteronomyst document is denoted by D; the one using Jehovah as the name of God, by J; the one using Elohim by E; the priestly document by P; and the Law of Holiness by H. JE is employed for the portions where J and E are inextricably intertwined.

thorship.[14] Where the subjects are the same and the ideas expressed differ, the author may have changed his mind,[14a] or he may have had different circumstances and conditions in view. Mohammed changed his views on marriage and other subjects and he changed the laws to suit his changing views. The condition of the Muslim changed after he went to Medina and especially after he set out to conquer the world; so he began to make new laws for his anticipated empire.

Nor, finally, is the language such as would indicate a time inconsistent with that of Moses. To be sure, there are in this particular document words and phrases which occur seldom, or never, elsewhere. But this is no proof of age or authorship but simply of subject, aim, and method. Nowhere else in the Old Testament is this subject of holiness fully treated. The aim of the writer is to secure the holiness of the people and he bases this holiness upon the holiness of God. Hence the frequent uses of the phrases: "I Jehovah am holy," "I am Jehovah," and "I am Jehovah which sanctify you." Since this holiness was to be secured by obeying Jehovah's law, we have the frequent injunction to walk in, or to observe and do, the statutes and judgments of Jehovah; and the threats of God's setting his face against them and of their even bearing their own sins and being excommunicated if they profaned his name, sanctuary, or sabbaths. As to words occurring in this passage alone, or infrequently elsewhere, this is characteristic of every document and almost

---

[14] Thus in the Koran, Mohammed refers five different times to the means by which Sodom and Gomorrah were destroyed. In two cases only is the language the same.

[14a] The clause "—the author may have changed his mind—" is unfortunate, for it is inconsistent with Dr. Wilson's high view of the inspiration of the Bible. The human authors of Scripture were superintended in their writing by the Holy Spirit so that what they wrote was what He desired them to write. They did not change their minds.

of every chapter of the Old Testament.[15] As to the claim that certain technical expressions[16] indicate a different author or age from that of the other documents of the Pentateuch, it is an assertion entirely unsupported by direct evidence and contrary to analogy.[17] That in the Law of Holiness the word for man should be repeated in the protasis in the sense of "whoever"[18] and that this phrase should occur eleven times in H and three times in P but not at all in JE or D is to be accounted for partly by the fact that JE and D are mostly in the second person and H and P in the third. Further, it is not clear that the idea of "whoever" as expressed by the repetition of the word for man is exactly the same as that expressed by other words and combinations. And lastly analogy shows that such variations are no necessary indication of different author or date.[19]

We have thus shown that in the peculiarities of H there is nothing opposed to its Mosaic authorship. But how about its authorship by another than Moses? Is it likely that a forger of a document would, scores of times, use phrases that occurred seldom, if ever, in the documents recognized as having been written by the author whose works he was

---

[15] See p. 108 f.

[16] Such as שאר, זמח and עמית (LOT 49).

[17] Thus the omen texts (or laws) published by Dennefeld *(Babylonisch-Assyrische Geburts-Omina,* Leipzig, 1914), have eleven words not found elsewhere to denote parts of the human body and about twenty other new words, or new meanings of words.

[18] איש איש.

[19] Thus in Dennefeld's *Geburts-Omina* there are five different ways of expressing the idea of "the one" and "the other." See his introduction, pp. 22, 23. The above remarks are based on the peculiarities of H as given in Dr. Driver's *Literature of the Old Testament,* pp. 49, 50. The same arguments which LOT uses to disprove the unity of the Pentateuch would disprove the unity of the Koran. We have in Mohammed's great work the same variety in the use of the names for God, duplicates, synonyms, contradictions, *hapax legomena,* and peculiar or favorite expressions. And yet all admit the unity of authorship of the Koran! See my article in PTR for 1919 on *The Use of "God" and "Lord" in the Koran.*

imitating? Would not the perpetrator of a pseudepigraph, intended to be accredited as a genuine work of the author whose name was falsely attached to it, have had the prudence or common sense to avoid as far as possible all indications of recognizable variations from the acknowledged originals of the man whose name he had attached? To attempt to prove a forgery by showing the alleged writer never existed, or that the dates of events, and peculiarities of language are wrong, is fair and according to the law of evidence;[20] but to expect us to believe that the forger of a document which was designed to be accepted as genuine should have made its language *differ* repeatedly, obtrusively and unnecessarily from that of another document by the author whom he is trying to imitate or personate, is contrary to common sense as well as to common law.

LAWS IN THE PENTATEUCH
ASCRIPTIONS

With regard to the remaining portions of the Pentateuch there is a strong presumption that they are the work of Moses; for we find that the collections of laws, however great or small these collections may be and whatever their subject matter, are in the E document attributed invariably to Moses. The so-called Code of the Covenant in Exodus 19-24 says in the prologue that Moses went up unto God in Mount Sinai and that the Lord said unto him: "These are the words which thou shalt speak unto the children of Israel" (19:2-6). So "Moses went down unto the people and spake unto them" (19:25) the words of chapter xx and the judgments of xxi-xxiii. Then in chapter xxiv we are told that Moses told the people all the words of the Lord and all the judgments (v. 3) and Moses wrote all the words of the Lord (v. 4) and afterward read the book of the covenant in the

---

[20] Compare Bentley's great argument against the genuineness of the Epistles of Phalaris in his *Dissertations upon the Epistles of Phalaris.*

audience of the people; and they said, "All that the Lord hath said will we do, and be obedient" (v. 7).

In like manner the Book of Deuteronomy is again and again ascribed to Moses. Thus it begins: "These be the words which Moses spake unto all Israel on this side of Jordan in the wilderness . . . in the land of Moab (vv. 1-5). Again, in the epilogue in 29:1, it is said: "These are the words of the covenant which the Lord commanded Moses to make with the children of Israel in the land of Moab, beside [i.e., apart from, or in addition to] the covenant which he made with them in Horeb."[21]

In P also the larger portions and the individual laws claim Moses as their author. Thus, the offering for the tabernacle and its plan were commanded by God to the people through Moses (Exod. 25:1,9 f.; 29:42,43). So also with the laws of offering (Lev. 1:1; 2; 7:37,38); of the consecration of the priests (Lev. 8:1,5,25,36); of unclean food (Lev. 9:1,46,47); of leprosy (Lev. 13:1; 14:54-57); and, in short, of all the other laws of the Pentateuch.

Now, with regard to any one in particular of these codes and laws, we do not see how any living man can have the assurance, the assumption of an impossible knowledge, to assert that it may not have been, as it claims to be, the work of Moses. Language, subject matter, and circumstances, all favor the claim of each particular section to have been what it professes to be. It is only by resorting to what we deem an unjustifiable method of procedure that any case can be made out on behalf of the deniers of Mosaic authorship. This method is based on the *presumption* that the documents are forgeries and that the writers were guilty of false

---

[21] In Deut. 4:1, we read: "Hear O Israel," where Moses is represented as the speaker. In 5:1, Moses "called all Israel and said unto them." In 27:1,11, Moses "commanded the people." In 31:1, Moses "went and spake to the people." In 31:24, it is said that "Moses made an end of writing the words of the law upon a book." Cf. also, 32:44,45, and 33:1.

statements as to the time and place and authors of the documents. Being utterly unable to substantiate these charges by direct evidence bearing on the separate documents, these deniers of Mosaic authorship resort to two expedients. They charge, first, that some of the documents contain numerous unnecessary repetitions, and that these repetitions are often incongruous; second, that these incongruities result from the fact that the documents represent widely different periods of development in the history of Israel.

REPETITIONS

Taking up these charges in order, it is admitted that there are numerous repetitions of laws bearing on the same subject, but it is denied that the repetitions prove that Moses was not the author. Every great teacher repeats. Every great reformer repeats. Witness Paul on the resurrection and on salvation by faith. Witness Mohammed on the unity of God and the condemnation of unbelievers.[22] The duality, or multiplicity, of authors cannot, then, be proved by the mere fact of repetitions.[23] Nor can it be argued from the fact that we cannot see the sense, or the reason, for the repetitions. Nor can it be argued from the fact that the repetitions are exactly alike, nor from the fact that they differ. Nor can diversity of authorship be argued from the fact that similar events are recorded as having occurred in the life of the same or different persons.[24]

To be sure, the critics make much of their inability to ac-

---

[22] Every sura of the Koran begins with the words: "In the name of the merciful and gracious God"; out of 114 suras 77 condemn the unbelievers by name and most of the others by implication.

[23] In the Koran, there are scores of parallels.

[24] All history and romance are full of such repetitions. Herodotus records several similar attacks on Athens by the Pisistratidae and two or more expeditions of the Persians against Greece. Caesar twice says that he built a bridge over the Rhine and that he sailed twice against Britain. Don Quixote and Don Caesar are full of repetitions. Everyone's life is full of them. So was that of Abraham; so was that of Moses.

count satisfactory to themselves for many of the differences and even adduce their ignorance of the reasons for them as if it were evidence against Mosaic authorship. And yet, good and sufficient reasons for most persons are evident in some of the repetitions. For example, take the laws with regard to the altar. Might not Moses (or at least Jehovah) have foreseen that it would be several hundred years before the worship at the central sanctuary could be established and that even afterward the union of the tribes might be disrupted, so that men like Elijah might not be able to go to the central altar to sacrifice even when they would? Could a God, or a law-giver, who provided for a second passover for those who could not attend the first, and permitted a pair of turtle doves, or even a handful of flour (a bloodless offering) to be given by those who were too poor to present a kid, not be expected to authorize an altar for special cases and circumstances?[25]

INCONGRUITIES

The second charge is that there are in the Pentateuch at least five principal documents representing different periods of time and different points of view; and that these differences of aim and time account for the alleged incongruities of the works attributed to Moses and exclude the possibility of Mosaic authorship. This charge is based upon the assumptions: (a) that Deuteronomy (D) was written in, or shortly before, 621 B.C.; (b) that the real, or alleged, incongruities between the parts of the Pentateuch can be explained only by assuming a wide difference of date in the time of their composition and a series of forgeries on the part of their authors.

DATE OF DEUTERONOMY

For the assumption that Deuteronomy was written in, or shortly before, 621 B.C. there is absolutely no direct evi-

---

[25] Cf. I Kings 3:2,3.

dence. The testimony of Deuteronomy itself is that it was given by Moses in the plains of Moab. The passage in II Kings 22-23 ascribes it to Moses (23:25). Josiah attributes the wrath of Jehovah to the fact that the fathers had not hearkened to the words of the Book that had just been found and read before him (22:8-13). Huldah, the prophetess, represents Jehovah as saying, I will bring upon this place all the words of the book which the king of Judah hath read (22:16). The elders of Judah and of Jerusalem and the king, and all the men of Judah and all the inhabitants of Jerusalem, and the priests, and the prophets, and all the people, both small and great heard the words of the book of the covenant which was found in the house of the Lord and covenanted to perform the words of the covenant that were written in this book (23:1-3). Although the Book of Deuteronomy contains laws affecting the king (17:14 f.) and the prophets (18:15 f.) and the priests (18:1 f.), and although it must be admitted that kings and prophets and priests had existed in unbroken succession from the time of Samuel down to the time of Josiah, and that the kings and prophets and priests must have had the customary laws and regulations, yet no protest against the genuineness and authenticity of the newly discovered book was made by king, or prophet, or priest. All accepted it as authoritative, and proceeded to carry its injunctions into execution (23:1-25).

Against this evidence of the documents themselves, the critics make the charge that the writers of the sources of II Kings 22-23, (that is "the book of the chronicles of the kings of Judah," cf. 23:28), the composers of the Books of Kings and Chronicles, and Hilkiah the high priest, Shaphan the scribe, Huldah the prophetess, and Jeremiah the prophet, were either forgers or dupes; and that Deuteronomy was not a work of Moses at all, but a composite work of an unknown author put together or at least promulgated for the purpose of deceiving the people into the acceptance of a great reform in worship. The kernel of this reform is affirmed to be the confining of the worship to the central sanctuary at Jerusalem. To be sure, the Book of Deuteronomy says nothing expressly about Jerusalem. Huldah, also, does not mention it as a central sanctuary (II Kings: 22: 15-20). The king and people, including prophets, priests, and scribes, do not specifically mention a central sanctuary in their covenant with Jehovah (23:3). Jerusalem itself is mentioned, it is true, in 23:23, as the place where the Passover was held; but according to the Books of Kings, the temple at Jerusalem was to be the dwelling place of Jehovah (I Kings 8:29; 9:3), in accordance with the promise made by God through Nathan to David (II Sam. 7:13). Jeremiah, who prophesied in the days of Josiah, speaks not merely of the fact that Jehovah had chosen Jerusalem to put His name there (7:11,14; 32:34), but also says that at the first Shiloh had been the place where the Lord had set His name (19:12). Not merely in the Pentateuch, but also thirty times in Joshua, once in Judges (20:17), sixty times in Samuel, and thirteen times in Kings, the ark is named as the center of the worship of the people of Israel. When this ark was removed to Jerusalem by David, and not till then, did the city become the place where men ought to worship (Jer. 3:16,17). Moreover, that Jerusalem was recognized as the place of the central sanctuary in the time of Solomon is clear from the fact that one of the first acts of Jeroboam, son of Nebat, was to appoint Bethel and Dan as rival centers, so as permanently to remove the people of Israel from the influence of the cult at Jerusalem (I Kings 12:28-33).

Thus neither for their general charge nor for their principal specification do the critics find any direct evidence in Deuteronomy or Kings nor in any other Old Testament document. Jeremiah, whose genuineness they acknowledge, is silent as to the general charge, but absolutely clear in his evidence against the specification with regard to the time of the organization of the central sanctuary. It is time for the body of intelligent Christian believers, who are deemed capable of sitting on juries in a court of common law, to assert themselves against these self-styled scholars who would wrest from them the right of private judgment. For in the settlement of this question no special scholarship is involved — no knowledge of Hebrew or philosophy. The English version affords all the facts. The evidence is clear. On the face of it, it is all against the critics. Only by throwing out the evidence of the very document on which they rely for the proof of their own theory and by placing a childish confidence in what remains, can they find any support for their destructive views.[26]

THE FOUR CODES OF LAW

The critics charge that the incongruities which they allege are to be found between the code of the covenant (E), and Deuteronomy (D), and the Law of Holiness (H), and the Priestly codex (P), are due to the fact that E represents the law as it existed prior to 700 B.C., D a law written about 621 B.C., H a law written about 600 B.C., and P a law written mostly before the events recorded in Nehemiah 8-10. Since the direct evidence of the documents themselves is against this fourfold date and ascribes all four documents to Moses, the critics have undertaken the difficult task of proving that these laws constitute a series of forgeries, extending over a period of about 500 years, committed by more than seventeen different persons, all reformers of the

---

[26] For good discussions of the origin of Deuteronomy, see Möller, *Are the Critics Right?*; Finn, *The Unity of the Pentateuch*; McKim, *The Problem of the Pentateuch*; Orr, *The Problem of the Old Testament*; and Green, *The Higher Criticism of the Pentateuch*.

highest ethical standards and all devoted to the service of Jehovah, the God of truth. Besides *mirabile dictu*, the forgeries were all successful in that prophets, priests, Levites, kings, and people, were all alike induced to receive them as genuine and to adopt them as obligatory, as soon as they were made known to them. The Jews and the Samaritans, the Pharisees and the Sadducees, the Rabbis, Aristeas, Josephus, Philo, Christ and the Apostles, all accepted the combined works as of real Mosaic authorship. But no amount of camouflage could deceive the critical eyes of the German professors and their scholars (all of whom agree with them; hence the phrase, "All scholars are agreed"). To them the imperfections of the codes and their disagreements, yes, even the particular half century in which each law was promulgated, are as clear as the spots on the sun, if only you will look through their glasses, and are not blinded by prejudice occasioned by faith in Jehovah, or Christ, or by the rules of evidence. Now, whether those who believe in Jehovah and Christ are blinded by prejudice, or not, it seems obvious that they who profess to believe in both cannot be expected without stultification to ignore the testimony of all the documents that Jehovah Himself was the real author of the laws, Moses being merely His mouthpiece, or prophet. This testimony cannot be set aside in the case of the laws without being set aside also in the case of the prophets. There is no more ground for calling it a form of speech in the one case than in the other. And if Jehovah did speak the laws and command the people to obey them, it must seem reasonable to suppose that He at least thought that they were harmonious. Christians, also, and professedly Christian professors need make no excuse for the prejudice that this testimony of the documents themselves is confirmed for them (however it may be with infidels) by the attestation of the New Testament writers and of the Lord Jesus Christ. But whether Christians or infidels, *we should all be bound strictly by a prejudice in favor of the rules of evidence.* Binding ourselves, then, to abide by the evidence, let us proceed to state the evidence for the defense in the case of the critics against Moses.

First, we find that in every one of the legal documents of Exodus, Leviticus, Numbers and Deuteronomy, the superscription as in Numbers 15; 19; 35; and in the case of all the longer collections such as Exodus 20-24; 25-31; Leviticus 1-7; 17-26; and Deuteronomy, and many of the smaller collections such as Exodus 12:1-28; 34; Leviticus 8; 13; 16; 27; Numbers 1; 2; 4; 6:1-21; 8:1-4; 5-22; 27:6-23; 28-30, the subscriptions also expressly attribute their authorship to Moses. In many cases the locality and the time in which these codes, or special laws, were given are specified. Thus, Exodus 12 was given in Egypt in the first part of the first month (vv. 1,3); Exodus 19:24, a Sinai in the third month of the first year of the Exodus (Exod. 19:1,11); Numbers 1:1, at Sinai in the first day of the second month of the second year after they came out of the land of Egypt; Deuteronomy, in the land of Moab, on the first day of the eleventh month of the fortieth year (1:1,3,5). In other cases as in Leviticus 17-26, and Exodus 25-31, the place at least is expressly stated. Here, then, are twenty separate documents all ascribed to Moses in the proper place and manner with dates and places affixed.

Second, we find that the variations in the form, treatment, and subject matter of the laws support the claim that Moses was the author. Some of the laws, as Leviticus 11-13, treat but one subject; others as Exodust 34 treat several subjects; and others as Leviticus 17-26 and Deuteronomy may be dignified with the name of code. Some of them as Leviticus 16 are so constructed that scarcely a verse could be omitted without marring the effect of the whole, whereas, others are composed of many parts, each distinct in its purpose, but all necessary to the carrying out of the laws of its remaining parts.[27] Moreover, the laws of the covenant of JE in Exodus 20-24 and the epitome in 34:1-26, and the codes of H and D are mostly a collection of short injunctions more or less disconnected and without specification as to how they are to be carried out, whereas the laws in P are generally entirely separated from other laws, are detailed in their regulations, and embrace many matters not discussed, or barely mentioned in the codes of JE, D, and H. To this difference in treatment and details corresponds also a difference in literary form. The laws of JE, D, and H are codal in form and resemble the prototype set by the code of Hammurabi in that they have lengthy prologues or epilogues, D and H containing at the end, just like the Babylonian code, a large number of curses upon those who should disobey their injunctions. The laws of leprosy vary from the other laws in accordance with the subject which they treat. As to the laws of P there is an analogy to the laws of leprosy in the birth-omens,[28] and we may infer from the frequent references of Nabunaid to the necessity of discovering the cornerstone of the temples originally built by Naram-Sin, Hammurabi, and others of his predecessors, that these temens or cornerstones contained detailed plans for the construction of the houses of the gods, corresponding to the plan of the tabernacle in Exodus 25-30.[29] The

---

[27] Again, the persons addressed differ. In the codes it is the whole people who are enjoined, whereas the laws of P affect ordinarily only certain classes of individuals, such as priests, lepers, and Nazarites.

[28] See the *Babylonisch-Assyrische Geburts-Omina*, by Ludwig Dennefeld, Leipzig, 1914.

[29] In King's *Letters and Inscriptions of Hammurabi* II, pl. 242, No. 107, we have the plan of the temple of Sippar at Jahrusum made during the period of the first dynasty of Babylon.

narrative in Exodus 36-40 of the manner in which this plan was carried out under the direction of Bezaleel is paralleled also in many respects by the account in the autobiography of the Erpa Tehuti, the director of the artificers of the temples, and shrines of Hatshepsut, who according to most Egyptologists was queen of Egypt two centuries before the times of Moses.[30] The form of the numeration of Numbers 1-4 bears many resemblances to those of the Annals of Tahutmes III.[31] The boundaries of the land given in Numbers 34 resemble closely similar forms in Babylon.[32] The form of the ceremonies of the day of atonement in Leviticus 16 may be compared with the Ritual of the Divine Cult,[33] and the laws of issues, jealousy, and the red heifer (Lev. 15; Num. 5;19) with the Ritual of Elmbalmment.[34] That minute directions for the conduct of sacrifices, similar to those in Leviticus 1-7, must have been in use among the Egyptians is evident from the Liturgy of Funerary Offerings found in the Pyramid Texts;[35] as also from the Liturgy of the Opening of the Mouth.[36] That detailed directions for the selection and clothing of priests like those in Leviticus must have existed among the Egyptians is to be seen in the Liturgy of the Opening of the Mouth,[37] and the form of the regulations of Leviticus has a parallel in the inscription of Agum-Kakrimi (1350 B.C.) which describes the dress of Merodach and Sarpanit (KB, III, I, 135 f.); and especially in the dedication cylinder of

---

[30] Budge, *The Literature of the Egyptians*, London, 1914, p. 145.

[31] Petrie, *History of Egypt*, II, 103 f.

[32] Hinke, *A New Boundary Stone of Nebuchadnezzar I*, and the tablet from the time of Hammurabi in KB, IV, 17. The Egyptians had boundaries for countries, nomes, and farms. See Breasted's *Ancient Records of Egypt*, V, 109, and Hinke's note in *A New Boundary Stone of Nebuchadnezzar I*, p. 9. See, also, King's *Babylonian Boundary Stones*.

[33] Budge, *op. cit.*, p. 248.

[34] *Idem* 247.

[35] Budge, *op. cit.*, 16.

[36] *Idem* 13.

[37] *Idem* p. 14.

Nabonidus containing the account of the consecration of his daughter as a votary of Nannar.[38]

We thus see that the various forms in which the sections of the law are preserved to us in the Pentateuch are paralleled in almost every instance by the forms of laws to be found in known documents of ancient Babylon and Egypt dating from 1000 to 4000 (?) B.C. And what in general is true of the form is true also of the contents of the laws. The civil and criminal laws of E, D, and H, bear a striking resemblance to those found in the Code of Hammurabi.[39] The moral precepts find their prototype and often their parallels in the maxims of Ptah-hotep (3000 B.C.), and in the moral precepts of chapter 125 of the Book of the Dead.[40] As to the ceremonial laws it can be claimed that the elaborate, lengthy, and intricate systems of worship centering around the numerous temples of the polytheistic Babylonians and Egyptians make the system of worship and religious observances enjoined in H and P seem in comparison models of clearness, simplicity, and ease in execution.

In the third place, the laws of Moses, as Emil Reich has so well argued,[41] demand a single great originator. Granting a great man like Moses, the prophetic mediator of God's ideas, and the fabric of the tabernacle, with the priesthood, and the sacrifices, and the sacred seasons, and the laws of holiness, and the covenants between the holy people and their unique God, rises before us as naturally as the constitution of the imperial Caesars from the mind of Augustus, or the religion of Islam from the life of the Arabian prophet, or the Christian Church from the life and death and pre-

[38] See *Miscellaneous Inscriptions in the Yale Babylonian Collection*, by Albert T. Clay, Vol. I, pp. 66-75.

[39] See especially Müller: *Die Gesetze Hammurabis*, and Kohler, *Hammurabi's Gesetz*.

[40] 18th dynasty or earlier. Budge, *Egyptian Literature*, 52, 22.

[41] *The Failure of the Higher Criticism of the Bible.* See, also, Naville's *The Higher Criticism in Relation to the Pentateuch.*

cepts of its Founder. It was the idea of God which Moses had that was the spring of his activities, the source and unifier of his thoughts and laws. No one can deny that the idea of a unique God was first obtained from the Israelites or that their literature always ascribes the first clear and full apprehension of this idea to Moses. How much of it he got from his meditations beneath the desert skies and how much by the direct revelation of the all-wise and all-powerful Jehovah, may be questioned; but that he had it, is the concurrent testimony of J and E and D and H and P and of all Jewish literature in legislation, history, and song. Prophets, priests, kings, poets, and people — all had this great idea, and all unite in saying that they derived it from Moses. And whatever Israelites were the first to be possessed with the Old Testament idea of an only God, let us remember that some Israelite certainly must have been thus possessed, seeing that the idea is to be found in ancient literature in the Old Testament and there alone. What more natural, then, than that the great thinker who first grasped the idea in its fullness should have found a revolution wrought in the whole system of his thinking. The universe with all its rolling years, the sun, the moon, the stars, the earth with its seas and islands, its plants and living creatures, must all be correlated to the great I AM, who made them all. And a greater than he has said that the law was ordained by angels through the hand of a mediator.

But the most engrossing subject of his thought must have been man in his relation to the earth and God and sin and death and redemption. And so he gathers up the history and the traditions of the past and centers the whole about the idea of a promise and the covenants, the covenant with Adam, the covenant with Noah, and the covenant with Abraham. And when God makes a covenant with the people of Israel through him as mediator he sets all his mind and energies to work to enable the people to observe their part of the covenant until the Star should arise out of Jacob and He whose right it is, that Prophet like unto himself, should come, whom Israel should hear, and to whom should be the obedience of the nations. And with this great thought in mind he sets himself to work to separate the Israelites from all the surrounding nations and from the polytheistic nations which had ruled them in the past. He takes the two great conceptions of natural religion, holiness and righteousness,[42] and seeks to separate them from their idolatrous associations and to raise them to a higher ethical and religious plane in the service of the one, ever-living, and true God.

As for a language and a literary form in which to express his thoughts, he did not have to invent them. They were already there.[43] All he had to do was to infuse new meaning into the old vehicles of thoughts, as in later times the New Testament writers did with the vocables of Greece, and Mohammed with those of the Arabs.[44]

As for the festivals, there were already plenty of them in use among the Babylonians and Egyptians and doubtless among the Israelites themselves — New Year, and New Moons, and Sabbaths. He simply had to take the old seasons and sanctify them to better purposes.[45] Sacrifices there also were

---

[42] קדש and צדק.

[43] We have shown this already for the form. As to the existence of the Hebrew language before the time of Moses, it is abundantly shown in the proper names of the inscriptions of the times of Hammurabi, Tahutmes III and Amenophis IV, and in the 111 common terms of the Amarna Letters. See Knudtzon, *Die El-Amarna-Tateln*, p. 1545 f., and W. Max Mueller, *Die Palästinaliste Thutmosis III.*

[44] E. g., in the case of *hanif*. The word *hanif* is Arabic, and means, "inclining to a right state," "inclining from a false religion to a true one," "inclining in a perfect manner to Islam and remaining steadfast therein." During the Time of Ignorance it applied to one who had made the sacred pilgrimage and was circumcised. Later it was applied to the Moslem who supposedly had turned away from belief in a plurality of gods to Allah. The root of *ḥanafa* means "to incline," "to decline."

[45] It is not meant that some entirely new festivals may not have been added.

and altars and priests. He brings them all into ordered harmony with his idea of holiness and righteousness in the service of Jehovah. Ethics there were. He gives them the sanction of the divine command, and approval. Customs there were, laws of clean, and unclean food, laws of jealousy, and revenge and disease and personal uncleanness, and fringes on garments, and tattooing, and vows and inheritances, and slavery and marriage. He brings all into his all-embracing scheme and makes them all subserve the one great purpose of bringing and keeping the people in obedience to their covenant God. Requirements and observances were multiplied until it was impossible for the people not to sin; but for the sins there was atonement and for the sinners, substitution, redemption and forgiveness, of a God that was long-suffering and gracious, plenteous in mercy, forgiving iniquity and transgression and sin, though he would by no means spare the guilty.[46]

Fourth, against this prima-facie case in favor of the Mosaic origin of the laws and against the life of Moses and the history of Israel as recorded in the books of Exodus, Leviticus, Numbers, and Deuteronomy, the critics bring a general charge and a number of specifications. The general charge is that the Pentateuch was not the work of Moses, but that it, together with the Book of Joshua, is a compilation of the works of seventeen, or more, authors and of laws and traditions of little historic value gathered together during a period of five or six hundred years from 800 or 900 B.C. to 300 B.C. Inasmuch as no claim is made in Genesis or Joshua that they are the works of Moses, we claim the privilege (without precluding or prejudicing the right of Moses to be considered the author of Genesis) of confining for the present discussion the defense of Mosaic authorship to the

---

[46] That is, those who refused the means of grace or willfully disobeyed his commands, like the man who gathered sticks on the Sabbath day, or Korah, Dathan, and Abiram.

four last books of the Pentateuch. And, as the charge involves the question of the authorship, as well as the much more important question of the historicity of the books we shall discuss first of all this fundamental question of authorship.

AUTHORSHIP. It must then be clearly defined what exactly is meant by Mosaic *authorship*. Certainly, it cannot mean that to be the author Moses must have written his literary works with his own hand. Else, would Prescott not be the author of the *Conquest of Mexico,* or Milton of *Paradise Lost,* or the kings of Egypt, Babylon, Assyria, and Persia, of their inscriptions, nor Jesus of the Sermon on the Mount. Lest this statement should seem too naïve, let us recall that a favorite and reiterated traditional argument of the critics against Mosaic authorship is based on the fact that it is not expressly said that he was charged by God to write anything but the curse against Amalek and an account of the wanderings in the wilderness (Exod. 17:14; Num. 33:2). Besides these small portions of the narrative, he is said to have written the code of the covenant in Exodus 20-24, and a portion at least of Deuteronomy.[47] In fact, it may reasonably be inferred from Deuteronomy 31:9,24-26; 4:44, 1,5; 28:58,61; 29:20,26; and other passages, that the whole Pentateuch, or at least all of the legal portions, was intended by the writers of these passages to have been designated as having been written by, or for, Moses.

But even if he did not write a word with his own hand, it is evident that whoever wrote the book meant to imply that the authorship of Moses extends to the laws and visions and commands which God gave to him in the same manner that the Code of Hammurabi was the work of the king whose name it bears. That is, the laws came through him and from him. This is the fundamental authorship for which we contend, and which we claim to have been unimpeached by

---

[47] See Dr. Green, *On the Pentateuch,* p. 37.

all the testimony that has been produced, in the endeavor to impair our belief that, as John says: The law was given by Moses.

The case then, as it stands, is as follows. The documents of the Tetrateuch state that Moses at expressly stated places and times wrote, or caused to be written,[48] certain parts of them. The critics charge that these statements of the documents are all false. What proof have they to substantiate this charge?

MOSES WROTE[48a]

First, they allege that "Moses wrote" in these passages is not a forgery, but simply a technical expression, or form of speech. But what evidence have they for this allegation? None whatever; but on the contrary, the evidence of the profane literature and of the other books of the Old Testament is all against it.

As early as the fourth dynasty of Egypt, documents are dated and the name of the authors given,[49] and in Babylon, as early as the dynasty of Hammurabi, documents are dated as to month, day, and year, and the names of the scribes and the principal persons engaged in the transactions recorded are given.[50]

In the Biblical documents also, it is the custom to give the author of the legislation. Thus in the Book of Joshua, the earlier legislation is invariably attributed to Moses,[51] and the new regulations are ascribed to Joshua himself.[52] So in Samuel, the old laws are ascribed to Moses and the new ones to Samuel.[53] So in Kings, Solomon regulates his kingdom

---

[48] The verbs may be pointed as Hiphil.

[48a] Moses wrote in alphabetic Hebrew. For a discussion of the origin and development of the alphabet see Appendix 2d.

[49] See Breasted's *Ancient Records of Egypt*, I, 891.

[50] See Schorr, *Urkunden des altbabylonischen Zivil- und Prozess-rechts.*

[51] 1:7; 20:2; 23:6.

[52] 24:26.

[53] I Sam. 8:6-22.

and Jeroboam the son of Nebat regulates the worship of
Israel with laws that are never ascribed to Moses, but to the
kings themselves, who are represented as departing in large
measure from the law of God already known (I Kings 8-11;
12:25-33; 14:7-16). So in Chronicles David divides the priests
and Levites and writes out the pattern of the temple. Jehoshaphat himself gives laws, and sets judges in the land,
and gives them charge as to their duties (II Chron. 19:5-11),
and proclaims a fast without reference to the laws of Moses;
and Hezekiah sets the Levites according to the commandment of David (II Chron. 29:25-27). In Nehemiah, the singers and the porters keep the word of their God according
to the commandment of David and of Solomon his son (Neh.
12:45).[54] Moreover, is it not marvelous that no example
has been found in pre-Christian literature of the ascription to Moses of a law not found in the Pentateuch? You
may be sure that if one such were known it would have
been proclaimed by the traducers of the unity of the Pentateuch with a blare of trumpets, for it would be the unique
specimen of direct evidence bearing on their alleged common use of the phrase to denote non-Mosaic authorship.
But no. Tobit has his hero burn the fish's liver at the command of an angel, not according to a law of Moses. The
Zadokite fragments never ascribe their additions to the
Pentateuchal laws to Moses. Therefore, let those who allege
that the phrase "the Lord said to Moses" is a legal fiction
produce some evidence or let the indictment of the claim
of the laws of the Pentateuch to Mosaic authorship be
dropped. Some later writer by mistake or intention surely
might have ascribed one law at least not found in the
Pentateuch to Moses. But no such ascription has been found.
No, not one.

---

[54] Whenever Chronicles and Nehemiah were written, their testimony shows
that the writer did not know anything about a legal fiction ascribing all laws
to Moses.

Again, we find that no law of the four books from Exodus to Deuteronomy inclusive is in the Pentateuch, or anywhere else in the pre-Christian Jewish literature, attributed to anyone but Moses. The modern critic asserts that the laws called Mosaic were not given by him but that they were written by at least seventeen different authors and redactors; and yet no one of these critics can mention the name of even one of these seventeen. To be sure, some of them have assumed that Hilkiah forged the portion of Deuteronomy which, according to the accounts in Kings and Chronicles (the only sources of our information on the subject) Hilkiah himself attributed to Moses. And we find that some have alleged that Ezekiel *may* have written the Code of Holiness in Leviticus 17-26, but unfortunately for the critics, Ezekiel who is never backward about affixing his name to his other works, abstained from doing so to the work under consideration.

Again some have asserted that Ezra may have written P or even have composed the whole Pentateuch; but here again they draw on their imagination for their facts, since the books of Ezra and Nehemiah both state clearly that Zerubbabel and Ezra and Nehemiah established in Jerusalem the laws and institutions that had been given by God to Israel through Moses.[55]

---

[55] Thus, according to Ezra 3:3, Jeshua and Zerubbabel built the altar, "as it is written in the law of Moses," and offered sacrifices and set the priests and the Levites in their offices "as it is written in the book of Moses" (6:18). According to Neh. 8:1,3, Ezra the scribe brought and read the book of the law of Moses, which the Lord had commanded to Israel. And in v. 14, we are told that they "found written in the law which the Lord had commanded by Moses" certain laws with regard to the feast of Tabernacles. In 9:3, it is said that the book of the law of God was read and it is acknowledged in v. 34 that the kings and princes and fathers had not kept the law. But the people covenanted (10:29) to walk in God's law which was given by Moses the servant of God. Again, in 13:1, we are told that "they read in the book of Moses." On the other hand, the service of song is said to have been reinstituted after the ordinance of David, king of Israel (Ezra 3:10).

WHERE MOSES WROTE

In the next place, all the laws of the Pentateuch attributed to Moses are either expressly, or impliedly, said in the record to have been given at certain *places,* that is, either in Egypt, or somewhere on the way from Egypt to the Jordan. This evidence, as to the localities in which the documents were written, so important in establishing the genuineness of any document, is almost absolutely ignored by the assailants of Mosaic authorship. What kind of lawyer would he be who attacked or defended the genuineness of a letter without considering whether the locality where it was written was mentioned and whether paper, ink, language, and contents, harmonized with the alleged place of its production? Now it is said that the following sections of the law were commanded in the localities cited, to wit: Exodus 12 in Egypt (Exod. 12:1), Exodus 19-24; 25-31; and 34, at the mountain; Leviticus 1-7, in the wilderness of Sinai; Exodus 19: 1,2,3,20; 24:12,13,16; 31:18; 34:2,29; Leviticus 7:38; 25:1; 26:46; 27:34; Numbers 1:1; 3:1; 9:1, out of the tabernacle of the congregation (Lev. 1:1). Others are preceded by the phrases: after they had left Egypt (Lev. 9:45; 22:33; 23:43; 25:55; Num. 25:41); from the camp (Lev. 24:33; Num. 5:2); when ye come into the land (Num. 15:2,18; 33:51; 34:2; Deut. 26:1; 27:2); while they were in the wilderness (Num. 15:32); in the plains of Moab (Num. 26:3,63; 27:3 [by implication]; 31:1; 36:13; Deut. 1:5; 29:1).

Now, the critics adverse to Mosaic authorship of the Pentateuch have been sharp enough to see that if they can throw doubt upon the accuracy of the documents with regard to these places, they will impugn the veracity of the accounts. So, after a hundred and fifty years of diligent search they find one apparent flaw. It seems that E and D use Horeb in place of the Sinai of J and P as the locality of the giving of the law. Horeb is said to be the designation of the mountain of God used in the northern part of Palestine where E is assumed to have been written and Sinai that used in Judah, where J and P were written. But the critics fail to attempt even to show why D, a document of the Southern Kingdom, should have followed E instead of J, and why P should have failed to harmonize this alleged discrepancy, or even to have remarked upon it. Perhaps, the simplest and most obvious explanation is the best. Horeb and Sinai were in a sense the same, just as the Appalachian chain and the Allegheny Mountains and Chestnut Ridge are the same. I was born near the Chestnut Ridge of the Allegheny Mountains of the Appalachian chain. In Europe I might speak of the Appalachian Mountains as my birthplace; in California, of the Alleghenies; in Western Pennsylvania, of the Chestnut Ridge. But I was born in only one place. So, as Hengstenberg long ago said,[56] "At a distance the mountain of God was called Horeb; near at hand, it was called Sinai, or once possibly Horeb."[57] The use of mountain before Horeb is no proof that it was a single eminence and not a ridge; for Mount Ephraim was "the hill country of Ephraim" or as *Hastings Dictionary* says,[58] "the mountain ridge in Central Palestine stretching N. to S. from the Great Plain to the neighborhood of Jerusalem."

---

[56] *On the Genuineness of the Pentateuch,* II, 327.

[57] Exod. 33:6, in a passage of which Dr. Driver said: "No satisfactory analysis has been effected," LOT, 38. In his work entitled *From the Garden of Eden to the Crossing of the Jordan,* Sir William Wilcox claims that Horeb and Sinai were both in the northern part of the peninsula and that the law was given from both. Prof. Sayce, also, puts both of them in the northeastern part of the peninsula. If Sinai is a part of Horeb the whole argument of the critics falls.

[58] Vol I, p. 727.

WHEN MOSES WROTE[58a]

But lastly, not merely are all of the documents of the Tetrateuch (with the exception of a few ascribed to Aaron) ascribed to Moses, and the place where most of them originated indicated, many of them are *dated* as to year, month, and day. The critics *quietly* ignore these dates. They would possibly attribute them to the cunning of the forger, and assert that they were inserted with the express purpose of giving to the documents in which they occur the appearance of verisimilitude. Think of a counsel arguing before a court that the fact that a document — a will, a contract, a letter, a check — was correctly dated was prima-facie evidence, not that it was genuine, but that it was a forgery! Let the critics show at least that the dates are not in the form of dates used in the time of Moses. But this they cannot do. But, on the other hand, it can be shown that in every particular the dates are of the same form as those that were used before 1500 B.C. There are two full forms of dates in the Pentateuch. The first gives the order of the day, month, year, as in Num-

---

[58a] The question of when Moses wrote is related to the dates of the exodus and conquest; between these dates (a lapse of forty years) the Pentateuch was probably written. Two principal views are held with respect to the date of the Exodus. The early view would date it about 1450 B.C. and the late view about 1290 B.C. Advocates of a late date appeal to the building activity in connection with Pithom and Raamses. These cities, it is claimed, were built under Ramses II, (1290-1224 B.C.). Furthermore, destruction of Bethel, Lachish, and Debir by fire is said to have taken place in the thirteenth century B.C. and this is identified with Joshua's destruction.

In support of the early date, appeal may be made to the chronology of I Kings 6:1 which puts the building of Solomon's temple 480 years after the Exodus. The beginning of the sojourn in Egypt is best placed before the Hyksos period, and not during that age. The building activities described in Exodus are not to be identified with the building activities of Ramses II who made of Raamses a capital. With respect to the destruction of the Canaanite cities, it should be noted that destruction by fire on Joshua's part was exceptional (only Jericho, Ai, and Hazor). Also, after Joshua's destruction the cities were reoccupied by the Canaanites. With respect to Hazor, destruction by fire occurred which would agree well with Joshua 11:13.

There are difficulties with respect to both views, but the earlier date for the Exodus appears to agree more closely with the Biblical data.

bers 1:1: "The first day of the second month of the second year after their going out from Egypt"; and the second, the order of the year, month, day, as in Numbers 10:11: "In the second year, in the second month, in the twentieth day of the month," and Deuteronomy 1:3: "In the fortieth year in the eleventh month on the first day of the month," and Numbers 33:38: "In the fortieth year of the going out of the children of Israel from the land of Egypt in the fifth month on the first day of the month." The distinguishing feature of these two systems of dating is that the former puts the year last and the latter the year first. The first system was used in Babylon and Nineveh from the earliest documents down to the latest, and the second system was used in Egypt in like manner from the earliest dynasties down to the time of the Ptolemies. Thus "in the month Ab, the twenty-second day, in the year after king Rim-Sin had conquered Isin";[59] "In the month Ayar, day 20, of the year after king Samsuiluna, etc.";[60] "In the month Shebat the fourteenth day, the second year after the destruction of Kiš"[61] [62] It will be noted that in every particular but one the dating of Numbers 1:1 is like the datings from the time of Abraham. This particular is that Numbers puts the day before the month. This, however, was a usual departure of the Hebrew writers in using the Babylonian system. Jeremiah 52:12 is the only place in the Old Testament where we find the order month, day, year. In Haggai 1:15; 2:10; Zechariah 1:7; and Ezra 6:15, all from postcaptivity times, we find the order day, month, year, as in Numbers 1:1. In all of these postcaptivity writings the name of the king is given exactly as we find it on the Babylonian documents from the time of

---

[59] Schorr: *Urkunden des altbabylonischen Zivil- und Prozessrechts*, p. 53.

[60] *Idem* 153.

[61] *Idem* 214.

[62] These kings lived in or about the time of Hammurabi. See, also, Schorr, pp. 279, 328, 416, for other examples.

Nebuchadnezzar II; whereas in Numbers 1:1, the dating is "after the going out of Egypt" just as in the earliest Babylonian documents.

Examples of the Egyptian system of dating are to be found in numerous places in Petrie's *History of Egypt*[63] in Breasted's *Ancient Records,*[64] and in the *Oxyrynchus Papyri.*[65] It is worthy of note, also, that the phrase "after the going out of Egypt" is paralleled in many cases in the earliest Egyptian records.[66] The Egyptian system is the one used commonly in the Old Testament by the writers who wrote before the return from Babylonia, and occasionally by those who wrote after 550 B.C. Thus we find the order year, month, day in Jeremiah 39:2; 12:4,31; Ezekiel 1:1; 8:1; 24:1; 29:1,11; 30: 20; 31:1; 32:1; 33:21; and Haggai 1:1; and the order year, day, month in Ezekiel 20:1; 26:1; 32:17; 40:1; Zechariah 7:1.

We see, therefore, from the above evidence that of the four full datings in the Pentateuch three follow the Egyptian system and one the old Babylonian. Of the three following the Egyptian system one is in the prologue to D[67] and two are in P.[68] The one in Numbers 1:1 follows the Babylonian order and belongs also to P. But the clause affixed (i.e., after the going out from Egypt) resembles the dates from the Hammurabi dynasty and not those from the time of Nebuchadnezzar or later. So that in respect to dates, as well as in respect to names and places, we find that the genuineness of the documents of the Pentateuch cannot be successfully assailed.

CONCLUSION

In regard to no one of these great prima-facie marks of

---

[63] E. g., II, 67, 100-103.
[64] E. g., I, 137, 139, 140, 145, 160.
[65] E. g., I, 170, 178, etc.
[66] Breasted, *loc. cit.,* I, 54.
[67] 1:3.
[68] Num. 11:11; 33:38; both assigned in LOT to P.

genuineness in documents — names, places, dates — have the destructive critics been able to show that the statements of the Pentateuch are false. As to these three specifications of the indictment, the assured result of scientific criticism, in strict adherence to the law of evidence, is that Moses gave the laws which have his name at the times and places indicated in the documents attributed to him as the mouthpiece of Jehovah.

II

THE EVIDENCE: Text

HAVING THUS SHOWN by three examples taken from the documents of the Pentateuch that from a prima-facie point of view these documents are substantiated by the evidence from the forms of contemporary documents and by the evidence as to their authors and as to the times, places, and contents of their composition, we shall proceed to consider the attacks of the critics upon the text, the grammar, vocabulary, and contents of the documents of the Old Testament, on the basis of whose "assured results" they seek to establish their reconstruction of the literature and history of the people of Israel.

In the remainder of this chapter and in the immediately following pages, I shall confine myself to the *text,* and shall endeavor to show that in view of the evidence bearing upon its origin and transmission the Hebrew text of the Masoretic Bible now in our possession is substantially reliable. In this and the succeeding discussions, I shall seek to follow without prejudice the laws of evidence as laid down in Sir James Fitzjames Stephen's *Digest of the Law of Evidence* insofar as these laws relate to documents. Where the evidence is already published and accessible to all, I shall merely refer my readers to the works containing the evidence. In cases where new evidence bearing on the subject can be produced I shall go more largely into particulars in order to show the grounds for my statements. As it will be impossible within the limits of a work such as this to give all the items of evidence, numerous citations of the sources of the testimony will be given; since it is the purpose of the writer to remove the discussion as far as possible from the field of subjective opinion to that of objective reality.

In the space at my disposal, it will be impossible to do more than suggest the reasons why I think that the charges against the general reliability of the Masoretic text cannot be supported by the documentary evidence, that is, by the "documents produced for the inspection of the Judges,"[1] and by the opinion of experts which may be called evidence as to what the evidence of the documents really is.[2]

TESTIMONY OF EXPERTS NECESSARY

The testimony of experts as to what the evidence really is

---

[1] See for this definition of "evidence," Sir James Fitzjames Stephen's work, *A Digest of the Law of Evidence*, p. 3. He defines evidence as "documents produced for the inspection of the Court or Judge." In this case of the critics against Mosaic authorship of the Pentateuch, every intelligent reader may consider himself the court and judge and jury.

The question may be raised why, if the intelligent reader can constitute himself court and judge and jury, the "critics" themselves do not accept the Mosaic authorship of the Pentateuch. The "critics" are intelligent men and capable. Why do they then maintain a position so contrary to what the Bible teaches? The answer, we believe, is that men who reject the trustworthiness of explicit statements in the Bible are men of their times who are influenced by the climate of opinion in which they live. Today that climate of opinion is hostile to accepting the Mosaic authorship of the Pentateuch, and many, it is to be feared, simply fall in line without ever having made a thorough study of the arguments for Mosaic authorship. The most important and compelling of these arguments, of course, is the testimony of Christ.

[2] The fact that a person is of the opinion that a fact in issue, or relevant or deemed to be relevant to the issue, does or does not exist is deemed to be irrelevant to the existence of such fact, except when "there is a question as to any point of science or art." When such a question arises, "the opinions upon that point of persons especially skilled in any such matter are deemed to be relevant facts."

is especially necessary as to all subjects requiring special study or experience, such as all matters of science and art.[3] "It is a general rule of evidence that witnesses must give evidence of *facts,* not of *opinions.*"[4] But "facts, not otherwise relevant, are deemed to be relevant if they support or are inconsistent with the opinions of experts, when such opinions are deemed to be relevant." "Whenever the opinion of any living person is deemed to be relevant, the grounds on which such opinion is based are also deemed to be relevant," and "an expert may give an account of experiments performed by him for the purpose of forming his opinions."[5]

In fact, in questions of philology and history it is the experiments, i. e., the investigations of the original sources, which afford the grounds for the opinions of the expert, that are the most important part of his evidence; for they give the facts on which his conclusions are based. If the experiments or investigations have been faulty, either from an incomplete induction of the facts, or from a wrong interpretation of them, the grounds, or reasons, or opinions, based on the facts will also be faulty.

IMPORTANCE OF A CORRECT TEXT

In the case, therefore, of a literary document the first fact to investigate and establish is the original text of the document, and the second is the meaning of that text. When the

---

[3] Science and art "include all subjects on which a course of special study or experience is necessary to the formation of an opinion." Persons thus qualified are called "experts." "The opinion as to the existence of the facts on which his [i. e., the expert's] opinion is to be given is irrelevant unless he perceived them himself."

[4] Italics in Stephen. He says further: "An expert may not only testify to opinions, but may state general facts which are the result of scientific knowledge." "The unwritten or common law of other states or countries may be proved by expert testimony." Genuine writings "may be used for comparison by the jury" or "by experts to aid the jury." "Experts in handwriting may also testify to other matters, as e. g., whether a writing is forged or altered, when a writing was probably made, etc."

[5] See Stephen's *Digest,* 100-112.

original text can be produced the correct interpretation of it is the principal matter, unless charges of interpolation are made. If, however, the original document cannot be produced, certified copies of the original, or copies approximating as nearly as possible to the original, may be introduced as evidence, and will have value for all parties to a controversy in proportion as they are recognized as genuine copies of the original. It is this fact that makes the question of the transmission of the text of the Old Testament fundamental to all discussions based upon the evidence of that text. Only insofar as we can establish a true copy of the original text shall we have before us reliable evidence for our inspection and interpretation. In regard to the Old Testament therefore, the first question to determine is whether we have a reliable copy of the original text. It is my purpose to convince my readers that the answer of experts to this question must be an unhesitating admission that in the text of our common Hebrew Bibles, corrected here and there, especially by the evidence of the ancient versions and through the evidence from palaeography, we have presumptively the original text. That is, we have it with sufficient accuracy to be reliable as evidence on all great questions of doctrine, law, and history. In support of this opinion, we shall in accordance with Section 54 of Stephen's *Digest,* give the following grounds, with the statement of the investigations on which they are based.

A. DIRECT EVIDENCE FOR TEXT

1. An examination of the Hebrew manuscripts now in existence shows that in the whole Old Testament there are scarcely any variants supported by more than one manuscript out of 200 to 400, in which each book is found, except in the use of the full and defective writing of the vowels.[6] This full, or defective, writing of the vowels has

---

[6] See collections of variants by Kennicott and DeRossi.

no effect either on the sound or the sense of the words. These manuscripts carry us back at least to the year A.D. 916, the date of what is probably the oldest MS. of any large part of the Hebrew Bible.[6a]

2.   The Masoretes have left to us the variants which they gathered and we find that they amount altogether to about 1,200, less than one for each page of the printed Hebrew Bible.[7]

3.   The various Aramaic versions (or Targums), the Syriac Peshitto, the Samaritan version, and the Latin Vulgate support with slight variations the present text.[8]

4.   The numerous citations in the New Testament, Josephus, Philo, and the Zadokite Fragments carry us back to the years A.D. 40 to 100. These citations show that those who used them had our present text with but slight variations. The numerous citations in the Hebrew of the Zadokite

---

[6a] This situation has changed greatly with the discovery of the Dead Sea Scrolls. See Appendix 2c.

[7] These variants are to be found on the bottom margin of the Hebrew printed Bible.

[8] See my comparisons of the Hebrew and Peshitto texts of Chronicles in *Hebraica*, Vol. XIV, 282-284. A comparison of the proper names of the Hebrew original and the Syriac version shows hundreds of variations of sight, largely between r and d, n and y, and k and b; hundreds more of variations due to sound, as sh and s, 'z and s, d and t, d and z, b and m, b and p, m and n, l and r, n and l, n and r (very uncommon), a, y, m, or r, or k, with gutturals, and palatals, interchanging in almost every possible way. One great peculiarity of the Peshitto is the frequency with which the proper names are translated and the large number of cases of the transposition of letters. This statement is based on a colletcion of the variation of the proper names of the Pentateuch, Joshua, Judges, Samuel, Kings, Chronicles, Ezra, and Nehemiah, made and possessed by myself in manuscript. There are over two thousand variants in this collection. The Samaritan Targum scarcely varies at all in sense from the Samaritan-Hebrew original. Its variants are mostly in the gutturals which are used almost indiscriminately. This statement is based upon a concordance made by myself with the assistance of Prof. Jesse L. Cotton, D.D., Rev. Robert Robinson, and Rev. C. D. Brokenshire. The variations of Jerome's version arose mostly from a vowel pointing different from the Masoretic. The textual variations of the Targums are similar to those of the Hebrew manuscripts and of the Masoretic readings. See Cappelus, *Critica Sacra* II, 858-892.

Fragments are especially valuable as a confirmation of the Hebrew text of Amos and other books cited.[9]

5.   The Septuagint version, the citations of Ecclesiasticus, the Book of Jubilees, and other pre-Christian literature, carry us back to about 300 B.C.[10]

6.   For the Pentateuch, the present Samaritan-Hebrew text (which has been transmitted for 2,300 years or more,

---

[9] Thus we find that the Zadokite Fragments cite the canonical books 226 times; 13 times from Gen.; 7 Exod.; 29 Lev.; 20 Num.; 23 Deut. (92 Pentateuch) ; 3 Joshua; 3 Judges; 6 Sam.; 2 Kings; 30 Isa.; 9 Jer.; 16 Ezek.; 9 Hosea; 2 Amos; 1 Obad.; 7 Micah; 1 Nah.; 3 Zech.; 4 Mal. (Minor Prophets 27) ; 13 Ps.; 1 Ruth; 10 Prov.; 3 Job; 1 Lam.; 1 Esther; 4 Dan.; 2 Ezra; 1 Neh.; 3 Chron. (That is, all the O. T. books except Ecclesiastes and the Song of Songs.) Some of these citations agree exactly with the consonants of our *textus receptus;* some differ slightly, some considerably; but they all indicate that the present text is substantially the same as that which was in existence when the book of Zadok was written. That Philo had the text of our Old Testament before him will be manifest to anyone who reads a page or two of Ryle's *Philo and Holy Scripture,* which gives Philo's citations from the canonical books of the Jews. For the New Testament, Toy's work on New Testament Quotations, shows plainly the same thing. As for Josephus, he himself claims that his *Antiquities* is based on the sacred writings of the Israelites and the writings demonstrate the truth of his statement.

[10] The differences beween the Hebrew Masoretic text and the Greek Septuagint are often grossly exaggerated. The vast majority of them arise merely from a difference of pointing of the same consonantal text. The real variants arose from errors of sight such as those between *r* and *d, k* and *b, y* and *w,* or from errors of sound such as between gutturals, labials, palatals, sibilants, and dentals, or from different interpretations of abbreviations. There is a goodly number of transpositions, some dittographies, many additions or omissions, sometimes of significant consonants, but almost all in unimportant words and phrases. Most of the additions seem to have been for elucidation of the original. In the case of Jeremiah we have in the Greek a recension which excludes many recurrent phrases. It may be compared with the Babylonian and Aramaic recension of the Behistun inscription as contrasted with the Persian and Susian. While substantially the same, they vary in many particulars.— For the Old Testament citations and allusions of Ben Sira, see my article on "The Hebrew of Ecclesiasticus" in the *Pres. and Ref. Review* for 1900.—For the Book of Jubilees, see the collection of variants by R. H. Charles in the *Apocrypha and Pseudepigrapha* of the Old Testament, II, 5, 6. Prof. Charles has gathered only 25 variants, 8 of single consonants, 1 of transposition of words, 9 of omission of a word and 1 of a phrase, 2 cases of change of gender, 1 of number, and 3 inexplicable corruptions. The result of his investigation is a wonderful corroboration of the substantial correctness of our present Hebrew text.

by copyists adverse to Rabbinical and Masoretic influences) agrees substantially with the received text of our Hebrew Bibles. Most of the variants are the same in character as those which we find in the transmission of all originals and especially in the transmission of our Hebrew text itself.[11] This carries the text back at the latest to about 400 B.C.

7. The Hebrew Scriptures contain the names of 26 or more foreign kings whose names have been found on documents contemporary with the kings. The names of most of these kings are found to be spelled on their own monuments, or in documents from the time in which they reigned in the same manner that they are spelled in the documents of the Old Testament. The changes in the spelling of others are in accordance with the laws of phonetic change as those laws were in operation at the time when the Hebrew documents claim to have been written. In the case of two or three names only are there letters, or spellings, that cannot as yet be explained with certainty; but even in these few cases it cannot be shown that the spelling in the Hebrew text is wrong. Contrariwise, the names of many of the kings of Judah and Israel are found on the Assyrian contemporary documents with the same spelling as that which we find in the present Hebrew text.

The names of Chedorlaomer and his confederates are written in the Hebrew as follows: Amraphel (אמרפל), Chedorlaomer (כדרלעמר), and Arioch (אריוך), Tidal (תדעל). The first name is undoubtedly meant to denote Hammurabi, king of Babylon, and is to be divided into *'ammu, rapi* and *ili*. The first syllable is usually written in Babylonian *ḥa*

---

[11] See Gesenius *De Pentatuchi Samaritani origine,* the standard work on this subject; and, also, the able criticism of the work of Gesenius by J. Iverach Munro, entitled, *The Samaritan Pentateuch.* See also a review of Petermann's *Pentateuchus Samaritanus* by R. D. Wilson in *Pres. and Ref. Review,* III, 199, and J. E. H. Thomson, D.D., *The Samaritans: their Testimony to the Religion of Israel,* and J. A. Montgomery, *The Samaritans.*

but there are cases where it is written *'a*.[12] The *l* at the end stands for *ilu* "god."[13] This word *ilu* is found at the end of the names of other kings of the same dynasty as Hammurabi, such as *Sumula-ilu, Samsu-ilu-na,* and also of persons not kings as *Šumman-la-ilu*.[14] The omission of the Aleph from אֵל ('el) is found also in Hebrew of the אָח ('ah) of Sennacherib and Esarhaddon. As to the names of the other kings, no one can deny that they are *spelled* correctly. For *Kudur* occurs in names of the time of Hammurabi[15] and *Laomer* occurs in Ashurbanipal's list of the gods of Elam.[16] The *Kudur-Lakhgumal* of Pinches inscription[17] is certainly the same as the *Kudur-Laomer* of Genesis 14. The changes

---

[12] See notes in King's *Letters and Inscriptions of Hammurabi*, LXVI and 253. The identification of Amraphel and Hammurabi must now be abandoned. For one thing Amraphel must be placed earlier than Hammurabi by some 300 years, and second, the two words are not etymologically related. What Dr. Wilson has written about Babylonian names ending in *-ilu* is of course correct, but there is no evidence to show that this applied to the great king. There are two points which rule out the identification; (1) The final *l* in Amraphel, and (2) the *u* vowel in the syllable *mu* in Hammurabi. If the Babylonian word were transcribed into Hebrew, we should expect it to be written as *ham-mᵉ-ra-bi* or *'am-mᵉ-ra-bi*.

[13] *Idem LXVI*. In British Museum Document No. 33212, *ilu* occurs before the name.

[14] King, *Letters, etc.*, III, pp. 21, 215, 241.

[15] King, *Idem* I. LV.

[16] See Streck, *Assurbanipal* II, 52. La-go-ma-ru (Annals VI. 33).

[17] KB II 205. In an article on the gods of Elam by M. H. de Genouillac in the *Receuil de Travaux*, 27, 94 f, we learn that the Elamite way of spelling the name was *La-ga-mar*, M. Francois Martin in his *Textes Religieux* gives the spellings as *La-ga-ma-al* (for which he cites two cases) and *La-ga-mar* (for which he cites two cases). Ashurbanipal spells the name *La-ga-ma-ru* (V. R. 6a, 33). The LXX gives it as Χοδολλογομόρ, having assimilated the first *r* to the following *l*. The name appears already in the time of Kutur-Nahhunti and again in an inscription of his brother, Shilhak-in-Shushinak. A son of Kutur-Nahhunti was called Shilhina-hamru-Lagamar (in three different texts), and Shutruru speaks of him as "the great."—King in his *History of Babylon*, p. 113, gives 2282 B.C. as the date of Kutur-Nahhunti (whose name he spells Kutur-Nankhumdi) and about 2080 B.C. as that of Hammurabi (*idem* 111). See also Scheil in the *Memoires of the Delegation en Perse*, Tome III, *Textes Élamites-Anzanites*, p. 49; and Deimel in the *Pantheon Babylonicum, Nomina Deorum, etc.*, Romae 1914, p. 160 f.

of the gutturals and palatals and of *l* and *r* are common ones in the transliterations of languages. Thus Babylonian *l* equals Persian *r*, Hebrew *l* equals Egyptian *r*;[18] Hebrew ע (ʿ) often equals Egyptian and Greek *g*, and Babylonian *ḫ*.[19] In Tidal the ע (ʿ) is regular for ח (*ḫ*), as in the first letter of Omri. In Arioch the consonants are exact equivalents of the like word in Sumerian. No one can doubt therefore, that the Hebrew text of the proper names may have been written in the time of Hammurabi; and that, whenever it was written, it has been handed down correctly to our times. The very disputes about these names are the very strongest corroborations of the general belief of all critics in the accurate transmission of the Hebrew text. In the twenty consonants of these four names we have, therefore, twenty witnesses to the correctness of the Hebrew textus receptus.

The five kings of Egypt are: Shishak (שׁישׁק), So (סוא), Tirhakah (תרהקה), Necho (נכו), and Hophra (הפרע), reigning at intervals from 1000 to 600 B.C. There are here 18 consonants in the Hebrew text and they represent 18 consonants in the cartouches of the kings named. Here we have one of the most remarkable instances of exact transmission of proper names on record. For first, the guttural consonants, א, ה, ח, and ע, the palatals and *r* all represent the same letters in the original. The only changes from the original are the assimilation of the *n* in Sheshank, the adding of the vowel letter ה at the end of Tirhakah, the changing of *sh* to *s* and of *b* to *w* in So, and the change of *b* to *p* in Hophra — all changes in harmony with the general laws

---

[18] In the case of *Laomer* the changes of *l* and *r* are found on the documents of Elam, Babylon, and Assyria.

[19] Thus עזה = Gaza in Greek and Gadatu in Egyptian. See Breasted, *Egypt* II. 179, Schrader in *Die Keilinschriften und das Alte Testament*, 107.3, 161.27, 256.3, and Knudtzon's *Die El-Amarna-Tafeln*, 289.17, 33, 40 (but also, *Azzati* in 296.32).

May not the Hebrew *Ayin* however also have represented the consonant *ġain* of Arabic? This would account for the *g* in such words as *Gaza* and *Gomorrah*.

of variations in sounds in the passing from one language to another.[20]

The kings of Assyria are Tiglath-pileser (תגלתפלאסר‎), Shalmaneser (שלמנאסר‎), Sargon (סרגון‎), Sennacherib (סנחריב‎), and Esarhaddon (אסרחדן‎); and the kings of Babylon Mero-dachbaladan (מרדךבלאדן‎), Nebuchadrezzar (נבוכדרצר‎), Evil-Merodach (אויל מרדך‎), and Belshazzar (בלשצר‎). These words contain 63 letters of which 59 are consonants. Comparing these consonants with those of the originals we find that the only changes in the Hebrew text contrary to general rules consist in the spelling Shalmaneser instead of Salman-ezer and the assimilation or dropping of *r* in the *sha(r)* of

---

[20] These statements about the names of the kings of Egypt mentioned in the Old Testament are based especially upon a study of the comparative values of the consonantal signs as exhibited in the inscriptions of Thothmes III on the gates of his temple at Thebes (Karnak). There exist still three lists of the cities of Palestine and Syria which Thothmes conquered. They have been edited and compared with the original Hebrew names, which they purport to render, by Prof. W. Max Müller of the University of Pennsylvania, in his work entitled *Die Palästinaliste Thutmosis III*. From these lists we gather the Egyptian way of expressing the Hebrew h, q (k), n, and r. Budge in his *First Steps in Egyptian* gives us on pages 9-11 the signs for ta, ka, sha (š), ab, ra'. Using the signs in the cartouches of the kings and comparing them with the letters used in our Hebrew Bible for spelling the same names we find that they are exactly equivalent except that the Hebrews according to their custom assimilate the n in Shishak, add the vowel h at the end of Torhakah, change the labials in Hophra and So and drop the ka in So. Taking up these varia-tions according to the apparent difficulty of explanation, we find that ka oc-curs in fifteen of the names of kings of Ethiopia (Petrie, *History of Egypt* III. 280-311). According to Brugsch, this ka is in Ethiopic the post-fixed article. If so, it would not be used in proper names in either Assyrian or Hebrew. The w in Siw' is changed from b as in Bath-Shu'a for Bath-Sheba. Sargon in Khor-sabad inscription I. 25, 26 calls him Sib–' .—e. The ' (א‎) at the end in He-brew is the proper vowel letter for the Egyptian vowel in ba.

In Hophra we have a *p* where the Egyptian has *b*. But the Greek of Herodo-tus has *p* and Manetho has *ph*. It is noteworthy that the Hebrew alone ren-ders correctly the gutturals ח‎ and ע‎. While the Hebrew text correctly keeps the ח‎ in the beginning the Targum has changed it to ה‎ the article and trans-lated the word as the unfortunate; the Syriac agrees with the Targum and renders by "the lame." The Hebrew kah at the end of Tishakah is certainly better than the Babylonian ku, the Hebrews having read the sign as ka and heightened the ă to ā at the end of the word and then written the vowel letter as usual.

Belshazzar.[21] As to the rendering of the Assyrian *sh* by *sh* it is to be noted that this is the way in which this particular root שלם is always written in both the Aramaic and Canaanitish dialects.[22] The writing in Daniel of Nebuchadnezzar for Nebuchadrezzar, involving the change of *r* to *n*, may be explained either by assuming that the former is the Aramaic form of the latter, or that the *r* is changed to *n* as in the example given in Lidzbarski.[23]

The four names of Achaemenid kings found in the Scriptures are Cyrus (כרש), Darius (דריוש), Ahasuerus (אחשורוש), and Artaxerxes (ארתחשסתא), of which the last part is written also ששת and ששתא. The *Aleph* in Xerxes is prosthetic as in the word *satrap* (אחשדרפן) and the final *Aleph* as found in certain spellings of the name Artaxerxes is *otiant*. The *Wau* in Xerxes is a contraction of *yama*. In the case of Artaxerxes the dental and sibilant are transposed in accord-

---

[21] For the latter compare the confusion of שמע and שמר by the Septuagint translators and the falling out or assimilation of *r* in the examples given in Lidzbarski's *Epigraphik*, p. 393. Compare also, the assimilation of the *r* to *l* in the Greek Chodollogomar; and also, the dropping of the *r* in the Assyrian transliterations of Egyptian names given in Assurbanipal's *Annals* I, 90-109, e. g., *Mimpi* for *Mn-nfr*, *Pisaptu* for *Pr-spd*, *Punubu* for *Pr-ub;* and the not infrequent change of *r* to *l*, or *l* to *r*, in the LXX, or the change of Egyptian *b* to *p*.

[22] This appears from numerous examples in Lidzbarski's *Epigraphik*, pp. 376, 377, for Phoenician, Punic, Hebrew, Nabatean, Palmyrene, and Egypto-Aramaic. For the *eser* the Assyrian has *asaridu*. Assyrian proper names were frequently shortened even to only one part out of three or more. See Tallquist: *Neubabylonisches Namenbuch* xiv-xxxiii. Compare, also, the Shalman of Hos. 10:14 and the Jareb of Hos. 5:13; 10:6; and the Nadinu of the Babylonian Chronicle (K. B. II. 274) for Nabu-nadin-zir. (Winckler: *History of Babylonia and Assyria*, p. 110.) If the full form of the name was Shalman-ašaridu-Ašur, the forms used in the Assyrian documents and in the Hebrew text would both be accounted for.

[23] *Epigraphik*, pp. 329, 393. See also my *Studies on the Book of Daniel*, p. 167, note. Since in Babylonia both *kuduru* and *kidinu* mean servant, it is possible that the latter was used by Jeremiah and Daniel to show that they interpreted *kuduru* as meaning servant rather than boundary. Again, both names might be shorter forms of Nabu-kudur-kidini-usur, "O Nebo, protect the boundary of the servant." Or, the *n* may be the Hebrew and old Aramaic (Nerab) form of the imperative with the *r* assimilated. Compare Note 21.

ance with general Semitic laws of dentals and sibilants. In the Sachau Papyri from the fifth century B.C. the names are written דריוש, כרש (or דריהיש, דריוהוש), השירש,, and ארתחשסש. In Babylonian the *Wau* in Darius is commonly written *m*, Xerxes has often a prosthetic vowel, and Arta-xerxes is written in the Babylonian recension of the original inscription Artaksatsu (or with an *ḥ* instead of *k*).[24] Thus we see that every one of the 22 consonants composing the names of the kings of Persia mentioned in the Bible has been transmitted correctly to us over a space 2300 or 2400 years. It may be added that in no other non-Persian document are they so accurately transliterated.[25]

---

[24] See Weissbach's *Keilinschiften der Achaemeniden*, and Strassmaier's *Inschiften von Darius* and numerous tablets in CT and VASD.

[25] Critics who hold that Esther and Ezra were not composed till after 300 B.C. and that both authors gained largely from Greek sources their information about the times which they describe will have a hard time explaining the way in which Xerxes is spelled in Ezra 4:6, and in the Book of Esther throughout. According to all known cases of transliteration, אחשורש cannot possibly be a transliteration of Xerxes. The X of the Greek is commonly transliterated in Hebrew, Aramaic, and Syriac by *ks* (כם) and infrequently by *ḳs* (קם); *ḥ* (ח) and *sh* (ש) being never used. Thus *Xerx* (for *es* is the Greek ending) could never become *'ḥšwrš*. [In Dalman's *Aramäisch-Neuhebräisches Wörtesbuch* there are nouns with כם and with אכם and with קם and with אקם corresponding to the Greek X or ξ, but not one with חם ,אחם, חש or אחש. The same is true of the Syriac words in Brockelmann's *Lexicon Syriacum*. On the other hand, if the writers of these lived in the fifth century B.C. in the Persian court, they could not have transliterated better than they have done. For Xerxes in Persian is *ḳšayarša*, the exact equivalent of חשורש, to which the Hebrew adds a prosthetic *Aleph*, as is done in the case of the Aramaic אחשרופ, *satrap* (Daniel 6:4) and אחשתרן *camel* (?) (Esther 8:10,14) and most commonly in Babylonian and also in the Syriac אחשירש (Peshitto of Esther 1:1), and Bar Hebraeus: *Chronicon Syriacum* p. 31 (Paris edition of 1890, sold by Maissonneuve). If we accept the Masoretic vowel pointing in Dan. 9:1 a Xerxes or Ahasuerus is referred to there also. If, however, we point as 'Oḥšaruš, we would have the Hebrew of the king of Media whom the Greeks called Cyaxares, and the Persians *uuakštra*. The name occurs in Persian only twice and both times in the genitive *uuakštrahyā* (Behistun §§ 24, 33)].

Artaxerxes, also, is in the Bible as exact a transliteration of the Persian way of writing the name, as is possible. The first part of the name is written in the Persian inscription *arda once (vase a)*, and *arta* nine times. The Elamitic follows the Persian even in the change of *d* and *t*; but Hebrew, Aramaic,

Other kings of foreign countries mentioned in the Bible and also on contemporary documents outside the Bible are Hazael (חֲזָהאֵל), and Rezin (רְצִין), of Damascus, Hiram (חִירֹם), and Ethbaal (אֶתְבַּעַל) of Tyre, Mesha (מֵשַׁע) of Moab, and Hadadezer (הֲדַדְעֶזֶר). These names contain at least 24 consonants, and every one of them has the proper writing in our Hebrew Bibles. In fact, Hadad (הֲדַד), and Ethbaal (אֶתְבַּעַל) are spelled more correctly in the Hebrew text than they are in the Assyrian records.[26]

Again, there are at least six kings of Israel and four of Judah whose names are found in the Assyrian records, to wit: Omri (עָמְרִי), Ahab (אַחְאָב), Jehu (יֵהוֹא), Menahem (מְנַחֵם), Pekah (פֶּקַח), Hoshea (הוֹשֵׁעַ), Azariah (עֲזַרְיָה), Ahaz (אָחָז), Hezekiah (חִזְקִיָּהוּ), and Manasseh (מְנַשֶּׁה). By comparing the Assyrian renditions of the letters it will be found that the whole 40 are written in our Hebrew Bibles in a

---

Babylonian and Greek always write *t*. The Persian *k* is always rendered by *k* in Elamitic and Greek (the first part of *ks*); in Babylonian it is represented by a *k* except in *vase a* where we have 'ḫ; in Hebrew and Aramaic we always have ḫ. The letter following *k* is in Persian on vase *a* К but everywhere else *š*; in Elamitic, Babylonian, Egypto and Biblical Aramaic and Hebrew, always *š*; in Greek the *s* part of *ξ*. The last syllable is in Persian *šКa* or the sign denoted by an *r* with an *s* over it and *a* following it. Elamitic denotes this syllable by *šša*, Babylonian by *ssu* (vases a, b, c) or tsu; Egypto-Aramaic by שׁסּ Biblical Aramaic by שׁתֻא (Ezra 4:7 *bis*, 8,11,23, vi. 14) and Biblical Hebrew by סֻתָא (Ezra 7:1,7,11,12,21; 8:1; Neh. 2:1; 13:6), the *s* and *t* being transposed in accordance with the general rule that where a dental comes before a sibilant the two consonants change places. Ezra 4:7 gives the whole syllable as *šta'*. The Greek gives the syllable *ξης*, transposing the letters *sk* into *ks* and adding the Greek ending *es*; but the *r* of the syllable *Xer* has no equivalent in Persian, or any other contemporaneous language. That *yama* should contract to *wau* (or ô) seems clear when we remember that *yama* is equivalent to *yawa* and that the *m* of Babylonian may change to *w* in West Semitic, as in *Saos* for *Shamash* in the name of the king Shamash-šum-ukin as given in Ptolemy's Canon. It appears from the above evidence that the Bible, especially in the whole writing of Ezra 4:7, presents the best transliteration possible of the original Persian name as spelled in the native inscription of the monarch himself.

[26] For a detailed discussion of the evidence see KAT and Lidzbarski's *Epigraphik.*

manner corresponding to the proper transliteration of Assyrian texts.[26a]

Thus we find that in 143 cases of transliteration from Egyptian, Assyrian, Babylonian and Moabite into Hebrew and in 40 cases of the opposite, or 184 in all, the evidence shows that for 2300 to 3900 years the text of the proper names in the Hebrew Bible has been transmitted with the most minute accuracy. That the original scribes should have written them with such close conformity to correct philological principles is a wonderful proof of their thorough care and scholarship; further, that the Hebrew text should have been transmitted by copyists through so many centuries is a phenomenon unequaled in the history of literature.

For neither the assailants nor the defenders of the Biblical text should assume for one moment that either this accurate rendition or this correct transmission of proper names is an easy or usual thing. And as some of my readers may not have experience in investigating such matters, attention may be called to the names of the kings of Egypt as given in Manetho and on the Egyptian monuments. Manetho was a high priest of the idol-temples in Egypt in the time of Ptolemy Philadelphus, i. e., about 280 B.C. He wrote a work on the dynasties of Egyptian kings, of which fragments have been preserved in the works of Josephus, Eusebius, and others. Of the kings of the 31 dynasties, he gives 140 names from 22

[26a] Since Dr. Wilson's day the names of two more Judean kings have been discovered in Babylonian and Assyrian records.

"On texts dating from the tenth to the thirty-fifth year of Nebuchadnezzar II [594-569 B.C.], the name of Jehoiachin has been found. These texts list deliveries of oil to individuals who are dependent upon the king, and Jehoiachin, 'the son of the king of Judah' is one of these dependents." (Cf. Pritchard, *op. cit.*, p. 308.)

"A building inscription of Tiglath-Pileser III mentions a *Ia-u-ḫa-zi* (Jehoahaz-Ahaz) who paid tribute. (Cf. Pritchard, *op. cit.*, p. 282.) There is also a carnelian seal which reads, "to Ushna, servant of Ahaz," (cf. Wright, *Biblical Archaeology*, 1957, p. 162) ."

The above two references are probably to King Ahaz.

dynasties. Of these, 49 appear on the monuments in a form in which every consonant of Manetho's spelling may possibly be recognized, and 28 more may be recognized in part. The other 63 are unrecognizable in any single syllable. If it be true that Manetho himself copied these lists from the original records — and the fact that he is substantially correct in 49 cases corroborates the supposition that he did — the hundreds of variations and corruptions in the 50 or more unrecognizable names must be due either to his fault in copying or to the mistakes of the transmitters of his text.[27] But, perhaps, the most striking example of the difficulty of transmitting accurately the proper names of kings, as well as the precariousness of using these lists as evidence against the Scriptures, is to be found in the lists of kings given by the astronomer Ptolemy in his *Canon*. Of the 22 kings that reigned over Babylon from Nabonassar to Nabunaid inclusive, Ptolemy mentions but 18; and of the 18 kings from Cyrus to Darius Codomannus, the names of eight are omitted.

This deficiency in the Ptolemaic *Canon* will be the more apparent when we observe that between the death of *Nergal-shar-uṣur* in 556 b.c. and the accession of Darius II in 424 b.c., i. e., in 132 years, the *Canon* gives the names and length of reigns of only six kings of Babylon, whereas the classics and monuments give the names, and in most cases, the approximate lengths of the reigns of nine others.

Now, Ptolemy and those who copied his *Canon* have been very careful in copying the notation of the number of years. It is different, however, when we look at the proper names. Thus, of the 18 names of the kings of Babylon from Nabonassar to Nabunaid, only the first and last, and that of Esar-

---

[27] Of the 27 kings of Egypt named by Josephus, only seven are spelled the same as in Manetho. Of the 41 kings of Assyria in the lists of Africanus, only one name is recognizable and it is misspelled. In Ptolemy's list of 18 kings of Babylon, only one is spelled exactly right. See my article on *Darius the Mede* in PTR for 1922.

haddon are written with approximate correctness. That their difference may be patent to the eye of our readers, I shall give the names in interlinear transliteration, the first line as given in the *Canon,* the second as we find the name on the Babylonian monuments:

1 Nabonassarou	2 Nadiou	3 Chinzirou kai Porou
1 Nabunasir	2 Nabu-nadin-zir	3 Ukinzir and Pulu
4 Iougaiou	5 Mardokempadou	6 Arkianou
4 Ululai	5 Marduk-aplu-iddin	6 Shar-ukin
7 Belibou	8 Apronadiou	9 Rigebelou
7 Belibni	8 Ashur-nadin-shum	9 Nergal-ushezib
10 Mesessimordakou	11 Assaradinou	12 Saosdoucheou
10 Mushezib-Marduk	11 Ashur-ahi-iddin	12 Shamash-shum-ukin
13 Xuniladanou	14 Nabokolassarou	15 Nabokolassarou
13 Kandalanu	14 Nabu-aplu-usur	15 Nabu-kudur-usur
16 Ilouarodamou	17 Nirikassolassarou	18 Nabonadiou
16 Amel-Marduk	17 Nergal-shar-usur	18 Nabu-na'id

Another example of the difficulty of transmitting proper names is to be found in the life of Alexander by the Pseudo-Callisthenes. Concerning this work the late President Woolsey of Yale College has truly said, that in the Greek manuscripts and in the versions "proper names assume different forms at will," and there is "an amazing difference in the proper names." "A daughter-in-law of Queen Candace is called Harpussa by B and C, Matersa by A, and Margie by V." "In the list of combatants in the games the Syriac has nine names like the Greek and Latin authorities, but they are all so much altered that two or three only have any resemblance.[28]

Thus we see not merely analogical evidence but the direct evidence of the documents forces us to the conclusion that the spelling of the proper names of the kings as given in the Old Testament must go back to original sources; and if the original sources were in the hands of the composers

---

[28] See for the evidence in full the article of President Woolsey entitled: "Notice of a Life of Alexander the Great" translated from the Syriac by Rev. Dr. Justin Perkins, New Haven, 1854, in Reprint from the *Journal of the American Oriental Society,* Vol. IV, 359-440.

of the documents, the probability is that since the composers
are correct in the spelling of the names of the kings they
are correct also in the sayings and deeds which they record
concerning these kings. And this we find in general to be
true where the Hebrew documents and the monuments both
record the great deeds of the kings. Thus the Hebrew Scriptures mention the expedition of Shishak against Judah, and
the Egyptian records at Thebes record the conquest of Judah
by the same king. The Assyrian monuments speak of the
wars of Tiglath-Pileser, Shalmaneser, Sargon, and Sennacherib; the Hebrew documents record the same events
generally in the same order and with the like results. Mesha
says that he asserted his independence of Ahab; the Scriptures say that he rebelled against Israel. From the mouths of
many witnesses — for in this case every consonant gives out
a voice of testimony — the Hebrew documents are corroborated. The great kings come up from the South and the
greater kings come down from the North, and the little
kings of Tyre and Damascus and Moab and Israel and Judah
meet them in the slash and clash of battle and the kings
record their victories on the pyla of Thebes, on the cliffs
of Behistun, on the stones of Moab, on the high built walls
of their palaces and tombs; and the great kings and the
small go alike the inevitable way of all flesh. But they did
not live in vain. For their deeds and their very names speak
out today in confirmation of the history of that little, oft
conquered, nation whose God was Jehovah and whose oracles
were the oracles of God.

8. The names of these kings — about forty in all — are
the names of men who lived from about 2000 to about 400
B.C., and yet they each and all appear in proper chronological
order both with reference to the kings of the same country
and with respect to the kings of other countries contempo-

rary with them. No stronger evidence for the substantial accuracy of the Old Testament records could possibly be imagined than this collection of names of kings. It means that out of 56 kings of Egypt from Shishak to Darius II, and out of the numerous kings of Assyria, Babylon, Persia, Tyre, Damascus, Moab, Israel, and Judah, that ruled from 2000 to 400 B.C., the writers of the Old Testament have put the names of the 40 or more that are mentioned in records of two or more of the nations, in their proper absolute and relative order of time and in their proper place. Any expert mathematician will tell you that to do such a thing is practically impossible without a knowledge of the facts such as could be drawn alone from contemporary and reliable records. When we consider that there are nine distinct lines of kings in the countries mentioned, and that there are several hundred kings in all, and that the length of the reigns of the kings could be determined only from the most accurate records, the chance of anyone who did not have access to reliable sources to get a record as exact as that preserved for us in the Hebrew Scriptures would be so small that no mathematician on earth could calculate it.[29]

9. The proper names and laws and customs of the time of Abraham are such as are met in the extra-Biblical records from the time of Hammurabi, of whom Abraham, according to Genesis 14 was a contemporary.[30]

---

[29] If there were 300 names of kings, each reigning 20 years, and 40 to be taken by chance, then, according to the algebraic rule that $n \ (n-1) \ (n-2) \ldots (n-r+1)$ equals the number of permutations, there would be one chance in about 75 x 1,000,000 to the sixteenth power of getting the names in the correct order. Even this chance would be made more impossible from the fact that the kings did not all reign an equal and synchronous period, but for periods of from one month to 66 years. See Wells' *Higher Algebra*, p. 362.

[30] See my article in the *Bible Student* for 1904. In reading the article please bear in mind that the proof was never revised by the author. See Appendix 2a.

Translations of many of these texts may be found in James A. Pritchard's *Ancient Near Eastern Texts Relating to the Old Testament*, Princeton, 1955.

10. The proper names and customs of the story of Joseph harmonize with the time when Joseph is said to have been in Egypt.[31]

11. The proper names of the Samaria ostraka and the names and events recorded on the Moabite stone agree with the Biblical records of the time of Ahab.[32]

12. Moreover, the kinds of foreign words embedded in the different documents of the Old Testament argue strongly for the genuineness and for the accurate transmission of this original text.

In order that the force of this kind of evidence may be fully appreciated, let me here say that the time at which any document of length, and often even of small compass, was written can generally be determined by the character of its vocabulary, and especially by the foreign words which are imbedded in it. Take, for example, the various Aramaic documents. The inscriptions from Northern Syria having been written in Assyrian times bear evident marks of Assyrian, Phoenician, and even Hebrew words. The Egyptian papyri from Persian times have numerous words of Egyptian, Babylonian, and Persian origin, as have also the Aramaic parts of Ezra and Daniel. The Nabatean Aramaic having been written probably by Arabs is strongly marked, especially in its proper names, by Arab words. The Palmyrene, Syriac, and Rabbinical Aramaic, from the time of the Graeco-Roman domination, have hundreds of terms introduced from Greek and Latin. Bar Hebraeus and other writings after the Mohammedan conquest have numerous Arabic expressions, and the modern Syriac of Ouroumiah has many words of Persian, Kurdish, and Turkish origin.

Now, if the Biblical history be true, we shall expect to find Babylonian words in the early chapters of Genesis and Egyptian in the later; and so on down, an ever-changing

---

[31] See Pinches, *The Old Testament*, etc., pp. 249-267.
[32] See Lyon in *Harvard Review* for 1911, p. 136.

influx of new words from the languages of the ever-changing dominating powers. And, as a matter of fact, this is exactly what we find. Thus, the first chapters of Genesis contain proper and common names of Sumerian or Babylonian origin,[33] and the Pentateuch has many Egyptian words.[34] In the time of Solomon, whose mother had been the wife of Uriah the Hittite and whose commerce included products from all countries, and whose empire extended from the Euphrates to the borders of Egypt, we find in the narrative words of Hittite, Indian, and Assyrian origin.[35] In the documents from the eighth to the sixth century we find predominantly foreign words of Syrian, Assyrian, and Babylonian character.[36] And in the records from the sixth century to the end we find Babylonian, Persian, and a few Greek words.[37]

13. The Old Testament documents claim that records were written by Moses,[38] by Joshua,[39] by Deborah,[40] by a young man of Succoth,[41] by Samuel,[42] by David,[43] and either

---

[33] E. g., Adam, Abel, Abraham, Arioch; and בהו ,תהום ,ברא (= Sumerian ba-ru [?], אד ,בנה (in sense of "form").

[34] E. g., Ramases, Pithom, On, Potiphar, Asenath; סין ,גמא ,תבה זרת ,סוף. It is now known that the word 'abrēk is Egyptian and means "pay heed." It consists of two Egyptian words, namely, ab (heart), and rek (to thee).

[35] Thus, שטם |and פרדם have their nearest analogies in Armenian, the closest of the Indo-Europeans to the ancient Hittites (see Meyer in Encyclopaedia Britannica, art. "Persia"). The names for apes and elephants (I Kings 11:22) are of Indian origin הב = iba (Burnouf Sanskrit Dict. p. 89), קפי = Kapi, (idem p. 140). And זבל, |and פחת ,סגן and היכל came from the Assyro-Babylonian (or from the Sumerian through the Babylonian).

[36] E. g., Hazael, Benhadad, Tiglath-Pileser, Merodach-Baladan, Bel, Nebo, Tartan, Rabshakeh.

[37] E. g., Zerubbabel, Sheshbazzar, Sanballat, and many names of officers, offices, and things are Babylonian, and the names of musical instruments in the Aramaic of Daniel are Greek. (See my article in Biblical and Theological Studies by the Faculty of Princeton Theological Seminary, p. 261, 1912.) On the Persian words, see Tisdale, *The Book of Daniel; Some Linguistic Evidence Regarding Its Date.*

[38] Thus, JE in Exod. 17:14; 32:82; 24:12; 34:17; D in Deut. 10:4; 4:13; 5:19; 10:2; 28:61; 31:9,22; P in Num. 33:2; Exod. 39:30.

[39] Josh. 8:32; 18:4; 24:26.

[40] Judges 5:14.

[41] Judges 8:14.
[42] I Sam. 10:25.
[43] II Sam. 11:14,15.

by, or in the days of, all the kings of Israel and Judah from Solomon to Zedekiah. For thousands of years before the time of Moses, the Egyptians on the southward of Palestine and the Babylonians on the east had been writing documents similar in form and content to those found in the Pentateuch. For thousands of years before Moses, the Babylonians had been making expeditions and carrying their culture to the coasts of the Mediterranean. For hundreds of years before his time, kings of Egypt had been raiding Palestine, and her merchants and travelers had been frequenting her ports and inland cities and leaving the records of their transactions in their tales and autobiographies. The Tel-el-Amarna letters, written to the kings of Egypt from every part of Palestine and Syria, show that writing in cuneiform was practiced everywhere in these countries 200 years before the time of Moses.[44] And the tablets from Taanach, Gezer, and elsewhere show that such writings were still made as late as 600 B.C. Various documents in Phoenician, Aramaic, Hittite, Cypriote, Cretan, Moabite, Minaean, Sabean, and Hebrew, from 1000 B.C. to 400 B.C., show that during all this period documents of various kinds were in use among the nations of western Asia in, and on every side of, Palestine. The character of the documents shows also that there must have been a general diffusion among the people of the ability

---

[44] That the Hebrew of the text may have been written as early as the time of Exodus is proved: (1) by the Hebrew words embedded in the Tel-el-Amarna Letters; (2) by the proper names in the Egyptian lists of places conquered in Palestine; and (3) by the proper names of the Hammurabi period. This evidence shows also that the forms of the noun and verb as found in Biblical Hebrew were already in existence. See Böhl, *Die Sprache der Amarnabriefe;* W. Max Müller, *Die Palästinaliste Thutmosis III;* Clay, *Light on the O. T. from Babylon,* p. 147; Ranke, *Early Babylonian Personal Names;* and Knudtzon: *Die El-Amarna Tafeln,* 1545-1549.

to read and write. In view of all these facts, the *sang froid* with which these modern critics and their followers affirm that writings could not have been produced among the Hebrews till 800 or 900 B.C. passes belief. Against the express and reiterated statements of the Biblical records that writing was in use among the Hebrews from Moses downward, supported as these statements are by all the direct evidence of the documents of all the surrounding nations, they set up their *opinion* — an opinion that receives no support from the documents, until they have been arbitrarily amended and interpreted in order to bring them into harmony with the *a priori* opinions which, on the face of them, the documents themselves clearly condemn.

B. EVIDENCE FROM ANALOGY

The testimony supplied by the history of the transmission of the text of other ancient documents, supported as it is by what we know of the transmission of the text of the Old Testament for the last 2,000 years, justifies the presumption that copies of the Old Testament text existent 2,000 years ago had in like manner been transmitted from their originals. Thus:

1. The fragments of classical writers found in the papyri of Egypt when compared with modern printed editions based on manuscripts, many of which are not a thousand years old, show that, with few important variations, the classical authors have been correctly transmitted for 2,000 to 2,500 years. In the fragments of 150 lines from Homer in the papyri from Oxyrynchus, the Fayum and Hibeh, edited by Grenfell, Hunt, and others, many lines are exactly the same as in the edition of Munro Allen. Most of the variants are merely slight such as adding *n*, or putting *e* for *ei*. In the two fragments of Herodotus, from the end of the third century A.D., published in the Oxyrynchus Papyri, there is

no variant from Dietsch's edition, though there are a few minor variations from Stein's edition.

2. The building inscriptions of Nabunaid refer to the fact that certain temples had been built by Hammurabi, who reigned over Babylon 1,500 years before his time, saying that he had found the *temens* or foundation stones of Hammurabi. In the copies of records of Hammurabi which were made about 650 B.C. for the library of Ashurbanipal, king of Assyria, and preserved in Nineveh, mention is made of the founding of these temples.[45]

3. The library of Ashurbanipal at Nineveh had thousands of documents that were copies of originals going back hundreds, and in some cases thousands, of years before his time.[46]

4. Some parts of the Egyptian *Book of the Dead* were in use in the same form for nearly 4,000 years.[47]

5. Scores of duplicates and triplicates among the Assyrian,

---

[45] See the *Keilinschriftliche Bibliothek* III, 11, 91, and King's *Letters of Hammurabi*, pp. 181-3. An inscription of Hammurabi in Sumerian says among other things: "When Shamash gave unto him Shumer and Accad to rule and entrusted their sceptre to his hands, then did [Hammurabi] build for Shamash, the lord who is the protector of his life, the temple Ebabbar, his beloved temple, in Larsam, the city of his rule." (King, *Inscriptions of Hammurabi*, p. 182.) In another inscription we read: "Hammurabi, the mighty king, the king of Babylon, king of the four quarters of the world, hath built Ebabbar, the temple of Shamash in the city of Larsam" (*idem* 183) . Referring to this temple Nabunaid says, that in his tenth year Shamash commanded him to restore Ebarra. He says that he found the *temen* and plan of the temple inscribed with the name of Hammurabi, "the old-time king who, 700 years before Burnaburiash, Ebarra and its Zikurat upon the old *temen* had built to Shamash. (KB. III. II. 0. Col. I. 54. II. 1-60, 1-32.) An inscription of Burnaburiash states that he restored the same temple of Ebarra. KB. III. II. 153.

[46] See Dennefeld, *Babylonisch-Assyrische Geburts-omina*, p. 9. 3, on the *Entstehungszeit, Entstehungs-und Ueberlieferungsart des Originalwerkes;* also, Hunger: *Beckenwarsagung bei den Babyloniern und Assyriern*, II. 503 f.

[47] A tradition as old as the twelfth dynasty says that chapter XXX B of the *Book of the Dead* was discovered by Herutataf the son of Khufu in the reign of Menkaura, a king of the fourth dynasty. It was cut in hieroglyphics and set under the feet of Thoth. This prayer was still recited by the Egyptians in the Ptolemaic period and so must have been in use for about 4,000 years. See Budge, *The Literature of the Egyptians*, p. 50.

Babylonian, and Egyptian documents show that from 2000 B.C. down to the year 400 B.C. copies of documents were often made with absolute exactness and generally with substantial accuracy.[48]

6. The variants in these duplicates show clearly, however, that differences in spelling, enumeration, and even omissions and additions, etc., are no proof in themselves of a difference in either age or authorship.[49] Examples of the different ways of spelling will be seen in the lists of Thothmes III at Karnak. Thirty-five variants occur in 119 names.[50] In the 17 lines of tablet No. 321 of Strassmaier's *Inschriften von Cyrus* the duplicate copy gives eight variants; one supplies an erosion, one an omission, one an explanation, three are corrections, and two fuller writings. One of the best exhibitions of duplicates and triplicates will be found in Dennefeld's *Geburts-Omina*. An intelligent study of this masterly work might well be made a propaedeutic to the study of textual criticism, illustrating as it does from numerous contemporary documents all kinds of copyists' mistakes due to sight and sound.

7. Hundreds of bilingual inscriptions containing the original Sumerian with its Assyrian translations, some made in the time of Hammurabi and some in the time of Ashurbanipal, as well as the four recensions of the Behistun in-

---

[48] Three of these duplicates may be seen in Strassmaier's *Inschriften von Cyrus* and 14 in his *Inschriften von Nebuchadonosor*. See also VASD. The five quadrilingual inscriptions of Darius on steles placed along the Suez Canal were duplicates, as were also his Egyptian inscriptions at El Khergeh. (See TSBA. V. 293 and *Recueil de Travaux* VII. 1, IX. 131, XI. 160.)

[49] This appears most clearly and frequently from the various originals of the Behistun inscriptions as they appear in the four recensions or editions, of which we possess one each in whole or in part in the Persian, Susian, Babylonian, and Aramaic. These differences will be discussed more fully when we come to consider the Book of Chronicles. Here attention is called merely to the fact that the Babylonian copy of the Aramaic varies frequently from its original in the enumerations, and that the Babylonian and Aramaic recensions are much shorter than the Persian and Susian.

[50] See plates in W. Max Müller's *Die Palästinaliste Thothmes III.*

scriptions, known to us, show that the kinds of variations that we find between the Hebrew text and its versions are to be found in them. As these variations do not impair the general veracity of these extra-Biblical documents nor militate against their antiquity or genuineness, so neither do the variations of the Hebrew text destroy their general and essential trustworthiness.[51]

8. If the original documents of the duplicates of the Old Testament (making about one-fifth of the whole) were written in cuneiform script, most of the variations between them could be paralleled by the variations in the translations of the Assyrian from the Sumerian.[52]

C. THE AD HOMINEM ARGUMENT

But the strongest argument against the critics from the textual point of view is the childlike simplicity with which they appeal to that part of the text which happens to suit their particular theory of Old Testament history, literature, or religion. After having, in order to prove this theory, cast out, without one item of evidence to support them, hundreds of words from the prima-facie text of the documents, they proceed to point and interpret what remains with as much assurance as if they had really proved beyond all contro-

---

[51] More than 2,000 interlinear texts are mentioned in Bezold's *Catalogue of the Cuneiform Texts in the Kouyunjik Collection of the British Museum.* Good examples are published in *The Seven Tablets of Creation* by Prof. L. W. King, pp. 130-139, 180. On page 217 of this same work will be found an example of a work in Sumerian containing word for word explanations in Assyrian. Hundreds of such texts have been found in the library of Kuyunjik (see Bezold's *Catalogue*, pp. 2010, 2092-2103). One of the most interesting of these bilingual inscriptions is by *Samsuiluna*, successor of Hammurabi, of which there are two copies of the Sumerian original and two copies of the Babylonian version, with slight variants in both originals and versions (see King, *The Letters of Hammurabi*, p. 198 f).

[52] E. g., the numerous synonyms in the parallel passages of Kings and Chronicles may be compared to the rendering of *DIM*, in the creation tablets, by *ba-ni, ba-na-at, ip-še-it,* and *e-pu-uš,* and *BA-RU* by *e-pu-uš,* and *ib-ta-ni.* See the *Creation of the World by Marduk* in King's *Seven Tablets of Creation,* I. 130-139. On this subject the author of this article read a paper at the International Congress of Orientalists in St. Louis in 1904.

versy that what they had arbitrarily cast out was false and with as much presumption as if they had actually proved that what they have retained is true. What would a court do with a plaintiff that desired to have a document admitted as evidence in support of his side of the case, after the same plaintiff had charged that the document was neither genuine, authentic, nor historical, and after the document had been amended to suit the contention of the plaintiff? Would the court not demand at least that the plaintiff should prove beyond controversy that the parts of the documents that the plaintiff desired to introduce as evidence were reliable as claimed? And since in almost every instance of such claim the critics are unable to produce any proof — simply because no such proof exists — is it not obvious that they must be debarred from introducing as evidence the parts that support their side, as long at least as they insist on denying the evidence of the parts that support the defense? In short, no argument can be made against that part of the text of the Old Testament which upholds the prima-facie evidence of the documents, which will not overthrow in a much greater degree the text that the critics attempt to establish.

D. CONCLUSIONS

In view of this mass of evidence, analogy, and admission, the following conclusions seem to be justified:

1. The traditional text has in its favor in the case of the most important of the documents the claim to have been in its original form written by, or for, certain definite persons and to have been written in the places and at the times mentioned; and the possibility of their having been written as claimed is supported by the outside evidence that writing was then in vogue, that the literary forms in which the text is written were then known, that the Hebrew language was then in use, that scribes and copyists were then existent,

that the contents are in harmony with what is *known* of the times when they claim to have been written.

2. The proof that the copies of the original documents have been handed down with substantial correctness for more than 2,000 years cannot be denied. That the copies in existence 2,000 years ago had been in like manner handed down from the originals is not merely possible, but, as we have shown, is rendered probable by the analogies of Babylonian documents now existing of which we have both originals and copies, thousands of years apart, and of scores of papyri which show when compared with our modern editions of the classics that only minor changes of the text have taken place in more than 2,000 years and especially by the scientific and demonstrable accuracy with which the proper spelling of the names of kings and of the numerous foreign terms embedded in the Hebrew text has been transmitted to us.[53]

3. From the above given array of evidence and especially from the fact that the destructive critics themselves make use of the traditional text in support of every theory which they have broached, the conclusion is irresistible that the textus receptus must be accepted in its prima-facie consonantal form as correct and reliable in all cases where there is no irrefragable weight of outside evidence, or at least of general analogy, against it.

4. In view of the thoroughly established fact that the vowel signs were not added to the consonantal text till about A.D. 600, and that the vowel letters were subject to change

---

[53] By *substantial* as used in the above statements we mean that the text of the Old Testament and of the other documents have been changed only in respect to those accidental matters which necessarily accompany the transmission of all texts where originals have not been preserved and which consequently exist merely in copies or copies of copies. Such changes may be called *minor* in that they do not seriously affect the doctrines of the documents nor the general impression and evident veracity of their statements as to geography, chronology, and other historical matters.

as late as the latest manuscripts, it results that all arguments based on specific vowel pointings must be abandoned, unless the pointings can be proved from outside evidence to be correct.[54]

5. In view of the exactness with which the proper names of persons and places have been transmitted for 4,000 years and their general agreement in the parallel passages, the presumption is, that the names for God, also, have been rightly transmitted. This presumption lays the burden of proof upon the critics, who, in order to establish their theory, arbitrarily and without any direct evidence in their favor, throw out *Elohim* from every place where it occurs in Genesis 2:3–4, and *Jehovah* from many passages in other parts.[55]

Finally, the analogy of the transmission of texts as shown among the Egyptians, Babylonians, Assyrians, Persians, Greeks, and Arabs, shows that there is a presumption against the theory of the critics that the Hexateuch is the result of the work of seventeen or more authors and redactors, com-

---

[54] Thus, Wellhausen's view in his *History of Israel*, p. 389, that *zakar* "male" was in earlier times *zakur* and that *zakur* must be substituted for *zakar* in Exod. 34:9; Deut. 15:19; and I Kings 11:15 seq.; and *zakar* read in all so-called later documents, is purely subjective and without any possible objective evidence in its favor. So, also, the pointing of אבד in Eccles. 3:6 represents merely the exegesis of the Masoretes and not necessarily the intention of the original writer. (LOT, 474). Objection to the arguments for the late date of Deuteronomy based on the use of *nathan* and *'asa* in 2:12, would be sufficiently met by pointing *nothen* and *'ose*. See discussion of the Masoretic vocalization in Appendix 1.

[55] The unjustifiable procedure of the critics with regard to the names of God is further shown by the analogy of the Koran, where we find the same variety in the use of the words for Lord and God that we meet with in the Pentateuch. This statement is based on a comparative concordance of *Allaha* and *rab*, which was prepared by me and published in the PTR for 1921. It shows that some Suras use neither, some one or the other, and some both; and this in all kinds of variations that are found in the Pentateuch. A phenomenon somewhat parallel to the usage of the divine names Elohim and Jehovah in Genesis appears in the texts from Ras Shamra. At times the god Baal is designated Baal, at other times, Aliyan and at still others Aliyan Baal. That the divine names are not sufficient criteria for distinguishing the identity of documents is being more and more recognized.

bining in an inexplicable and inextricable confusion, three or four parallel accounts and four, or more, recensions of laws representing widely different periods of time and development.[56]

---

[56] The analogy of the great historical work of Herodotus and of great works of fiction like *Don Quixote*, or Victor Hugo's *Don Caesar*, is convincing that duplicates such as are found in the Pentateuch are true to life. The biographies, also, of Thothmes III and Tiglath-Pileser I and Alexander and Caesar are as full of similar events as are those of Abraham and Moses. Caesar's accounts of his two voyages to Britain and of his two bridges over the Rhine are beautiful examples of them. Alexander was always consulting his *mantis*. "Lives of great men all remind us."

III

THE EVIDENCE: Grammar

Passing from the text to the grammar we find that in this line of attack upon the Scriptures, the latest evidence is also against the critics.

THE ABSTRACT FORMATIONS IN *ûth*, *ôn* AND *ân*

In one of the standard introductions to the Old Testament[1] the assertion is made that the use of "the frequent abstract formations in *ûth*, *ôn* and *ân*" in the Book of Ecclesiastes is among the proofs "so absolutely convincing and irrefutable" of the late date of the work, "that as Delitzsch exclaims: 'If the book of Koheleth be as old as Solomon, then there can be no history of the Hebrew language.'" Since Prof. Cornill here cites Delitzsch as his authority, let us rule Cornill out of court as giving hearsay evidence and address ourselves to what Delitzsch says.[2] He was one of the greatest Hebrew scholars of his generation, and fifty years ago his testimony on a matter concerning the history of the Hebrew language was as good as possible. But a history of the Hebrew language was in his time not possible. Gesenius, Ewald, Delitzsch, Keil, and all those brilliant scholars of the nineteenth century are as much behind the

---

[1] Cornill, *Introduction to the Canonical Books of the O. T.*, p. 449.
[2] In his *Commentary to Ecclesiastes*.

87

times today as expert witnesses to the history of the Hebrew language as Prof. Langley would be in Aeronautics, or a surgeon of the Civil War in comparison with a professor in Johns Hopkins. For since Delitzsch wrote the above, the Tel-el-Amarna Letters, the works of Hammurabi, the Hebrew of Ecclesiasticus, of the Zadokite Fragments, and of the Samaria Ostraka, the Sendschirli inscriptions, the Aramaic papyri and endorsements, and thousands of Egyptian, Babylonian, Assyrian, Phoenician, Aramaic, Palmyrene, Nabatean, Hebrew, and other documents throwing light on the Old Testament and its language have been discovered. These documents prove that the old-time alleged histories of the Hebrew language were largely subjective and fallacious; and that the presence of words with endings *ûth, ôn,* and *ân,* is no indication of the age in which a document was written.

Thus as to *ûth,* or *ut,* we have abundant evidence to show that it was common in every one of the four great Semitic families of languages except Arabic, where the unborrowed form is seldom found.[3]

For example, in Assyrio-Babylonian, there are three of them in the seven creation tablets,[4] six in the letters and inscriptions of Hammurabi,[5] thirteen in the Code of Hammurabi,[6] 13 in Dennefeld's omen tablets,[7] 15 in the Amarna Letters,[8] 18 to 20 in the inscriptions of Tiglath-Pileser I,[9] two in the incantations published by Thompson,[10] and ten

---

[3] Wright in his *Arabic Grammar* gives four examples of forms of words with this ending. See Vol. 1, p. 166. These four and four others, *rahabut, rahamut, subrut,* and *tarbut,* are certainly derived from the Aramaic. In a few cases, such as *ragrabuth, salabut,* and *darbut,* no Aramaic, Hebrew, or Babylonian equivalent has been found.

[4] King, *The Seven Tablets of Creation,* pp. 252, 254, 262.

[5] King, *The Letters and Inscriptions of Hammurabi,* 259-296.

[6] R. F. Harper, *The Code of Hammurabi,* 147-191.

[7] *Babylonisch-Assyrische Geburts-Omina,* 220-232.

[8] Winckler, *Tel-el-Amarna Letters,* 1-34.

[9] Lotz, *Die Inschrift Tiglath-pileser's,* I, pp. 204-218.

[10] *The Devils and Evil Spirits of Babylonia,* II, 165-179.

in the astrological tablets of the same editor.[11] These inscriptions were written from 2000 B.C. to about 625 B.C.

In the pre-Christian Aramaic we have five words with this ending in the Sendschirli inscriptions from north Syria of about the year 725.[12] The Aramaic portions of Daniel and Ezra each have four and the Sachau Papyri four or five.

In the Old Testament we find from 41 to 55 words of this form.[13] These forms are found in every one of the 24 books of the Hebrew canon except the Song of Songs, Ruth, and Lamentations. Unfortunately for the argument that the ending denotes lateness, nine of these words occur in Isaiah, 18 in Jeremiah, seven in Proverbs, seven in Samuel-Kings, one in Hosea and one in Amos, two in Ezekiel, two in Deuteronomy, two in H, and four in JE. Of the documents that some or all critics place after the captivity, Ezra has two words ending in *ûth*, Nehemiah three, Chronicles three, Haggai one, Daniel one, Job one, Psalms five, P two, Esther one, and Ecclesiastes five or six.[14] Joel, Jonah, Malachi, Ruth, the Song of Songs, Lamentations, and the parts of Zechariah, Proverbs and Isaiah, placed by the critics in post-captivity times have no words with this ending.[15]

In all the Biblical documents claimed as postexilic by the critics, the only words with this ending, not occurring in exilic or pre-exilic documents, and found in documents

---

[11] *The Reports of the Magicians and Astrologers of Nineveh and Babylon,* II, 113-152.

[12] מלכו, כברו, זכרו, אלהו, אברו.

[13] Fifty-five, if we count the forms in *ûth* from verbs whose third radical was *waw* or *yodh*.

[14] Of these words the only ones not found in the documents which the critics place before the Exile are עַבְדוּת (Ezra and Nehemiah, הַתְחַבְּרוּת (Dan. 11:23), חַלְמוּת (Job 6:6), אַיָּלוּת (Ps. 110:3; Eccles. 11:9,10), מַלְאֲכוּת (Ps. 73:28; and Haggai 1:3), and הוֹלֵלוּת, סִכְלוּת, שַׁחֲרוּת and שִׁפְלוּת in Ecclesiastes.

[15] The words ending in *uth* in Isa. 40-60 occur in 41:12; 49:19; 1:1,3 and 54:4. All of these passages are put by Duhm and Cheyne in the original work of Deutero-Isaiah. (LOT, p. 245.) Proverbs 30 and 31, according to Dr. Driver, "doubtless of postexilic origin," have no words ending in *uth*.

alleged by anyone to be from the Maccabean times are   ילדות
youth (Ps. 110:3),[16] התחברות *league* (Dan. 11:23), and
four words in Ecclesiastes.

Ecclestiasticus (180 B.C.) has four words in *ûth* not occurring in Biblical Hebrew[17] and the Zadokite Fragments (A.D.
40) have two.[18]

It is evident, therefore, that this ending is no proof of
the date of a Hebrew document, nor in fact of a document
in Babylonian, Assyrian, or Aramaic. The ending simply
denotes *abstract* terms. In the account which Bar Hebraeus
gives of the life of Mohammed, he has but one abstract ending in the account of his active career and seven in the account of his doctrine.[19]

So in the Bible the books treating of concrete events,
whether early or late, have but one or two of these words;[20]
whereas those treating of more abstract ideas have more
words with this ending whatever the date.[21] JE, the earliest
part of the Pentateuch, according to the critics, has four
words ending in *ûth*,[22] whereas P, the latest part, has only
two.[23]

---

[16] Cheyne puts this psalm in Maccabean times. Christ according to Matt.
20:44; Mark 12:36; and Luke 20:42; and Peter according to Acts 2:34, ascribe
it to David in terms as explicit as language can employ. Matt. 22:44 introduces
the citation from Ps. 110 by saying: How then doth David in spirit call him
Lord? Mark 12:36 says: For David himself said by the Holy Ghost. Luke 20:42
says: David himself saith in the Book of Psalms. Last, in Acts 2:34 Peter, in
his great sermon on the day of Pentecost says: For David is not ascended into
the heavens: but he saith himself, The Lord said unto my Lord, etc. Reader,
what think ye of Christ? Whose son is he? What think ye of the Holy Ghost?
Was Peter filled with Him? (Acts 2:4.) See further in my articles on the
Headings of the Psalms in the PTR for 1926.

[17] תמהות, גברות, בהלות, אבלו.

[18] עשרות and עריות.

[19] See the *Chronicon Syriacum*, Paris, 1890, pp. 97-99.

[20] Josh. two, Jud. one, I Sam. two, II Sam. two, I Kings two, II Kings two,
I Chron. two; II Chron. three; Ezra two; Neh. three; Dan. one.

[21] Thus, Prov. has seven, Isa. nine, Jer. eight, Eccles. six (Ecclus. eleven).

[22] מלכות put אלמנות, כבדות, עדות.

That Hebrew nouns ending in *n (nûn)*, i. e., the forms in *ôn* and *ân*, should be considered late is even less justifiable than in the case of *ûth*. For there are about 140 of such nouns in Hebrew occurring in all ages of the literature; and they are found, also, in Babylonian, Assyrian, and Arabic, as well as in New Hebrew and Aramaic. Besides in many cases, as in שלחן the nouns cannot have been derived from the Aramaic, simply because they have been found in no Aramaic dialect of any age.[24]

THE USE OF THE HEBREW TENSES

Leaving the morphology and coming to the syntax, we find that here also the critics of the Old Testament cannot support their charges by the evidence. The charge that the *Hebrew perfect forms* of the verb employed in Exodus 15 and Deuteronomy 1 show that these chapters were written after the conquest of Canaan, breaks down when we learn that Hebrew perfects are often equivalent to English future perfects, or even to an emphatic future.[25]

Again it is charged that the frequent use of *wau conjunctive*[26] *with the perfect* in Ecclesiastes is a proof that the book is one of the latest in the Old Testament. The discovery of the Hebrew of Ben Sira has broken the force of this argu-

---

[23] עדות found also in JE. and ממלכו in Josh. 13:21,27,30,31 a word found also in Hos. 1:4; I Sam. 15:28; II Sam. 16:3, and Jer. 36:1. The opinion of Delitzsch was probably founded on the numerous occurrences of this ending in the version of Onkelos, where there are 60 or 61 nouns with this ending (see Brederick's *Konkordanz*).

[24] For a further discussion of these endings, see p. 118 f. The following words, occurring in Ugaritic, are probably abstract nouns ending in *-ûth; abynt,* and *plṭt.* The following probably correspond to Hebrew nouns in *-ạn; zbln, hrsn,* and *qltn.* In addition a number of proper names end in *-n.* With respect to *schulchân,* it is interesting to note that *ṭlhn* occurs in the Ugaritic texts.

[25] Called in Hebrew grammars the perfect of certainty.

[26] The Hebrew forms perfect and imperfect refer to the character of the action as regards completeness and not as to time. The Hebrew conjunction *Wau* or *w,* usually with a change of accent and vocalization, has the power of changing the sense of a perfect to that of an imperfect, or the sense of an imperfect to that of a perfect.

ment; for we find that in it the *wau conversive* is used with the imperfect 120 times and 33 times with the perfect as against only five examples of *wau conjunctive* with the perfect. Moreover, the Zadokite Fragments have *wau conversive* with the imperfect 85 times and with the perfect 35 times, as against *wau conjunctive* 16 times with the imperfect and only three times with the perfect.

Again the critics have failed to explain how the use of this construction in Ecclesiastes can be due to the *time* when the work was written in view of the fact that Daniel which they put at about the same time as Ecclesiastes has about 200 cases of *wau conversive* with the imperfect and 75 with the perfect, and only five of *wau conjunctive* with the perfect. Again, if the use is due to the time, why is it that it is found only in Ecclesiastes and not in the so-called Maccabean psalms and the numerous other documents which the critics assert to be late? Again, how explain its presence twice in Judges 5 which many critics consider to be the earliest document in the Old Testament; or that the perfect occurs with *wau conjunctive* in Numbers 23, 24 seven times, to two times with *wau conversive*? It will not do to attempt to invalidate this explicit testimony of Ben Sira, the Zadokite Fragments, Daniel, and the writings alleged by the critics themselves to be from definite periods by saying that it is impossible otherwise to bring some of the uses of Ecclesiastes within the period of some critic's definition of what were the limits of use in good Hebrew for the perfect with *wau conjunctive;* for the probability certainly is that whoever wrote Ecclesiastes knew more about those limits than any of our modern professors. Shades of Jean Paul, Carlyle, and Walt Whitman! Ye could not have written in the nineteenth century, for no other mortals wrote like you.

THE SYNTAX OF THE NUMERALS

Whatever may be the explanation of the Priestly Document's use of the phrase "a hundred of" instead of "a hundred,"[27] it is certainly no indication of the *age* of the document nor of an authorship different from that of J, E, D, and H.

Starting out with the thesis that "statistical data besides genealogies are a conspicuous feature" in the narrative of P,[28] the critics in order to sustain their thesis violently and without any evidence ascribe nearly all of the passages containing the word for "hundred" to P, with the result that the word occurs according to their claims 50 times in P, and only five times in E, twice each in J and D, and once in H. Of these 60 cases, one in J, three in E, one in D, and one in P occur before *wau*, where the use of the construct state would be of course impossible. Ruling these out as having no bearing on the discussion, we have remaining 49 cases in P, two in E, and one each in D, H, and J. The example in H where the construct *me'ath* is found before *mikkem* is accounted for by the fact that the genitival relationship might have meant "your hundred" instead of "a hundred of you." The case in J (Gen. 16:12) cannot indicate the age of the document, since the same phrase occurs nowhere else in the Old Testament.[29] Of the two cases assigned to E, the one in Joshua 24:32 is a citation from Genesis 33:19. This verse is one of four (Gen. 33:18,19,20; and 34:1) which the critics, without any support from manuscripts or versions, or elsewhere, arbitrarily divide into six different portions. The word *keshita* which occurs here and in the citation in Joshua 24:32 is found nowhere else except in

---

[27] I. e., of the use of the *construct,* (מאת) instead of the *absolute* (מאה).

[28] LOT, 127.

[29] That is, followed by שערים, the phrase meaning "a hundred-fold." The only analogy to this is in II Sam. 24:3 (parallel to II Chron. 21:3) "a hundred times"; but in these passages פעמים is used.

Job 42:11. In combination with the word for *hundred* it occurs only in Genesis 33:19 and in the citation of it in Joshua 24:32. The only instance remaining outside of P is that in Deuteronomy 22:19 where it speaks of "one hundred [pieces of] silver." This is paralleled exactly only in Judges 16:5.[30]

Of the 49 cases where the word *hundred* is used in P, 22 are in apposition or the absolute state, as in "a hundred sheep," while 27 are followed by the genitive, as in "a score of sheep." Of the former, four may be ruled out (Exod. 27:9,18; 38:9,11) because they are followed by the preposition ב (b), one (Exod. 27:11) because it is followed by an accusative of specification, one (Num. 7:86) because it stands at the end of the sentence, and one in Numbers 2:24 because it stands absolutely for "a hundred." Of the remaining 15, 13 stand absolutely, the term for shekels having been omitted; so that only two cases are left where the common genitival construction (with מאת) might have been used. These occur in Genesis 17:17 and 23:1, places in P where "hundred of" could possibly have been used instead of "hundred." In both of these cases it is used before the noun for year, which is remarkable, because P usually (17 times in all[31] employs "hundred of." P also has "hundred of" three times before *talent*,[32] four times before the word for *thousand*,[33] twice before day,[34] and once before *base*.[35]

---

[30] In Judges 17:2 we have an example similar to that in Deut. 22:19 except that the definite article is used before the word for silver. In Neh. 5:11 the word מאת is used before the noun for silver accompanied by the definite article.

[31] Gen. 5:3,6,18,25,28; 11:10,25; 21:5; 25:7,17; 35:28; 47:9,28; Exod. 6:16,18,20; and Num. 33:39.

[32] Exod. 38:25,27[2] (twice with the article). As to the use of ככר we find it as early as II Sam. 12:30; I Kings 9:14,28; 10:10,14; 16:24; 20:39; II Kings 5:5,22,23[2]; 15:19; 18:14[2]; 23:33[2]; and as late as I Chron. 19:6; 20:2; 22:14[2]; 29:4[2],7[4]; II Chron. 3:8; 4:17; 8:18; 9:9,13; 25:6,9; 27:5; 36:3; Ezra 8:26[2] Esther 3:9. With מאה it is used in I Kings 9:14; 10:10; II Kings 23:33; II Chron. 27:5; 36:3.

[33] Num. 2:9,16,24,31. Before אלף we find מאה I Kings 20:29; II Kings 3:4[2]; I Chron. 5:21; 21:5; 22:14; 29:7; II Chron. 25:6.

Outside of P, *hundred* before the noun is found in Joshua one time, Judges four, J one, E two, D one, I Samuel two, II Samuel four, I Kings five, II Kings four, Isaiah two, Ezekiel ten, I Chronicles six, II Chronicles four, Ezra two, Esther three, i. e., 24 times in the literature preceding the Exile, 12 in Isaiah 40-66 and Ezekiel, and 15 in the post-exilic books.[36] "Hundred of" is used only three times in the postexilic books.[37]

The extra-Biblical evidence is as follows:

The Mesha inscription in Moabitic, which is a form of Hebrew, has the phrase, "a hundred of cattle" (מאתנקרין). The date of this inscription is the early part of the ninth century B.C. The Siloah inscription from about 700 B.C. has the phrase "a hundred of cubit."[38] Unfortunately neither construction is found in Ben Sira, nor in the Zadokite Fragments. In the Egyptian *Pyramid Texts* the numeral preceded the noun; but in the records of about 1530 to 1050 B.C. the numeral is put before the noun in the genitival construction.[39] In the *Tel-el-Amarna Letters, me-at* (= · מאת) occurs twice; once in 25.10 before *eru* "copper" and once in 19.39 before *lim* "thousand."[40] We thus see that the earliest Hebrew records and the Egyptian and Babylonian documents nearest to the time of the Exodus support the prevalent use of "hundred of" as we find it in P.

---

[34] Gen. 7:24; 8:3.

[35] Exod. 38:27.

[36] מאה is used elsewhere as follows: before רכב (II Sam. 8:4; I Chron. 18:4); פעמים, (II Sam. 24:3; I Chron. 21:3); אמה, (I Kings 7:2; Ezek. 40:19,23,27, 47² 41:13²,14,15); (42:8); נביאים(I Kings 18:4); איש (I Kings 18:13; II Kings 4:43; Judges 7:19; 20:35); שנה (Isa. 65:20²); כסף (Judges 16:5; 17:2 [with article]); Deut. 22:19; צמיקים (I Sam. 25:18; II Sam. 16:1); צאן (I Kings 5:3); מדינה (Esther 1:1; 8:9; 9:30); ערלות (I Sam. 18:25; II Sam. 3:14); שערים Gen. 26:12 (J); and קשיטה Gen. 33:19; Josh. 29:32 (E).

[37] Neh. 5:11; II Chron. 25:9; Esther 1:4.

[38] See Lidzbarski, *Nordsemitische Epigraphik*, pp. 106, 114, 416, 439.

[39] Erman, *Aegypten*, 63, and *Aegyptische Grammatik*, § 142, 122-126.

[40] Winckler, *Tel-el-Amarna Letters*, pp. 48, 80.

But neither do the critics have support in the later Semitic documents for their theory that the use of "hundred of" before the noun indicates lateness for the document in which it occurs. In Syriac the numeral stands in apposition either before or after that which is numbered.[41] The Biblical Aramaic and the inscriptions and papyri afford no examples affecting the question.[42] The New Hebrew follows the Biblical usages.[43]

From all the above testimony it is evident that there is no basis in the use of the word for "hundred" for concluding that P may not have been written by Moses.

THE EXPRESSION: X THE KING

The charge is made that the Hebrew of Daniel "resembles not the Hebrew of Ezekiel or even of Haggai or Zechariah but that of the age *subsequent to Nehemiah*." One of the alleged proofs of the charge is that in Daniel 1:21 and 8:1 the name of the king *precedes* the title. That this order is a proof of lateness in Daniel is affirmed in the words: "So often in post-exilic writings, the older Hebrew has nearly always the order   (דוד) המלך, 'the king David.' "[44] The following tables will give the number of times the orders

---

[41] See examples in Nöldeke, *Syriac Grammar*, § 237.

[42] מאה is used three times in the *Sachau Papyrus*, but always as a noun in the sense of the Roman "century," or company of a hundred men.

[43] Siegfried u. Strack, *Neuhebräische Grammatik*, § 73.

[44] LOT, 506. The inscription of Ariyaramna (c. 610-580 B.C.), contemporary with the earlier years of Daniel, which was first published in 1930, just one year before Dr. Wilson's death, admirably substantiates Dr. Wilson's argument. It begins, "Ariyaramna the great king," and a few words later continues, "says Ariyaramna the king." The last sentence of this short inscription also begins, "Says Ariyaramna the king." Another inscription which may be from Cyrus the Great or from the younger Cyrus reads, "I am Cyrus the king the Achaemenid." This is the pattern which was set for the later Persian practice, and with this pattern Daniel is in perfect agreement. The text is found in Roland G. Kent: *Old Persian Grammar Texts Lexicon*, New Haven, 1950.

"the king X" and "X the king" are used in the books written before or after 550 B.C.

	Before 550 B.C.			After 550 B.C.	
	The king X	X the king		The king X	X the king
I Sam.	1	1	I Chron.	4	9
II Sam.	10	2	II Chron.	15	9
I Kings	29	2	Ezra	2	2
II Kings	14	2	Neh.	0	2
Isaiah	6	0	Haggai	0	2
Jere.	10	2	Zech.	0	1
Eze.	1	0	Esther	9	0
	—	—	Dan.	0	2
Total	71	9		—	—
			Total	30	27

Since 12 of the citations from Chronicles are in parallel passages in Samuel-Kings, the 30 instances of the phrase "the king X" in the later writings may be reduced to 18; so that the proportion will be: "The king X" 71 to 18, "X the king" 9 to 27. The evidence, therefore, that the order "X the king" is often used in postexilic writings and that the order "the king X" is nearly always used in the older Hebrew" amounts to a mathematical demonstration. But a demonstration of what? Why, of the minute historical accuracy of Daniel, Haggai, Zechariah, Chronicles, Ezra, and Nehemiah, and of the unassailable character of the sacred Scriptures. For mark you, the early writings before 550 B.C. follow the Egyptian order "the king X,"[45] and the later writings follow the Babylonian and Persian order "X the king."[46] In Haggai 1:1,15; Zechariah 7:1; Ezra 7:7; 8:1; Nehemiah 2:1; 5:14; and Daniel 1:21; 8:1; we have exact copies of the Persian and Babylonian order.

Again, it is a matter of wonder that the author of the "Literature of the Old Testament" should have used this

[45] See the scores of examples in my article on "The Titles of Kings in Antiquity" in the PTR for October, 1904, and January, 1905.

[46] See the numerous examples given in the articles just referred to. For the Persian Kings *cf.* especially my articles in the *Sachau Denkschrift* (Berlin, 1912) and the PTR for January, 1917.

particular testimony to prove that Daniel did not resemble Haggai and Zechariah but was "subsequent to Nehemiah"; for the books of Haggai, Zechariah, Ezra, and Nehemiah all use the exact phrase which is produced as evidence that Daniel is later than they. Besides, the critics have not produced a single example from the Hebrew literature which they place in the age subsequent to Nehemiah to show that the form "X the king" was used by the Jews subsequently to Nehemiah. Neither Ben Sira nor the Zadokite Fragments have it;[47] nor does it occur in Isaiah 24-27; Jonah, Joel, Ecclesiastes, nor in any of the Psalms, nor in the Book of Proverbs. Nor in this case can the critics resort to the subterfuge of asserting that Daniel is late because the passages in Ezra and Nehemiah in which the phrase occurs are insertions into the genuine works of Nehemiah; for unfortunately for them, the phrase in every case appears in the parts of Ezra and Nehemiah which they themselves admit to be genuine.[48]

Reader, if the most plausible, and probably the most scholarly, of all that school of modern critics that delight to assail the integrity of the scriptural narratives and to use so frequently the modest appellation, "all scholars are agreed," will make such palpable blunders in a matter as to which there is abundant evidence to show that the Scriptures are right, what dependence will you place on him when he steps beyond the bounds of knowledge into the dim regions of conjecture and fancy? If, when we can get abundant evidence, the documents of the Bible stand the

---

[47] The nearest to it is the phrase "Nebuchadnezzar the king of Babylon" in the Zadokite Fragments, pp. 1, 6.

[48] Thus Ezra 7:7; 8:1 are in the so-called second section of Ezra embracing chapters 7-10 as to which Dr. Driver says: "There is no reason to doubt" that it "is throughout either written by Ezra or based upon materials left by him" (LOT, 549). The phrase occurs in Neh. 2:1; 5:14. Dr. Driver says: "Neh. 1:1-7: 73a is an excerpt to all appearances unaltered, from the memoirs of Nehemiah" (LOT, 550).

test of genuineness and veracity, and the charges of the critics are proved false, upon what ground of common sense or law of evidence are we to be induced to believe that these documents are false or forged when charges absolutely unsupported by evidence are made against them?

THE INFINITIVE WITH THE PREPOSITIONS *b* AND *k*

One more charge of the critics in the sphere of syntax will be considered because it covers several books and because it is reiterated in LOT.[49] It is that Daniel's and the Chronicler's use of the infinitive with the prepositions *b* "in" and *k* "as" indicates a date subsequent to Nehemiah. Two specifications are made; first, that this type of sentence is rare in the earlier books, and second, that the earlier books place the infinitive clause later in the sentence. Two witnesses only need to be called to answer these assertions. First, Ezekiel. He wrote between 592 and 570 B.C.[50] and his prophecies were "arranged evidently by his own hands."[51] His book is the one document of the Old Testament that the critics accept in its entirety, their theories being built largely upon it. Now, in this book there are 49 instances where *b* alone is used with the infinitive in the early part of the sentence, just as in Daniel and Chronicles, let alone those where *k* is used.[52] Since Ezekiel was written before 570 B.C., 35 years before we claim that Daniel was written, why is the use of the phrase seven times[53] by Daniel a sign of a date subsequent to Nehemiah 440 B.C.? The second witness we shall call is Ben Sira, who wrote about 180 B.C., just about 16 years before the month of June, 164 B.C., when some critics assume

[49] E. g. pp. 506, 538.

[50] LOT, 278.

[51] *Idem* 296.

[52] To wit, 1:17[2],18,19[2],21[3],24,25; 3:18,20,27; 5:16; 10:16[2],17[2]; 12:15; 15:5; 16:34; 18:24,26; 20:31[2]; 21:34; 23:37; 24:24; 26:15,19,27,33; 28:25; 29:7; 32:15; 33:8, 13,14,18,19,33; 38:14; 42:14; 43:8; 44:19; 46:10[2]; 47:3,7.

[53] To wit, 8:8,23; 10:9; 11:4, and 12:7.

that Daniel was written. In the 62 pages of the Hebrew as it is found in Smend's edition (57 in Strack's) we have but six sure examples of this usage, as compared with seven in the 10 pages of the Hebrew of Daniel, and 49 in the 85 pages of Ezekiel. That is, Ben Sira has about 10 per cent of one example per page as against 60 for Ezekiel and 70 for Daniel.[54]

---

[54] These two witnesses should be sufficient to convince anyone that the charges in LOT about the infinitive with *k* and *b* are false. However, if anyone is yet unconvinced, I have made a complete concordance of all the examples of the use of the infinitive with *b* and *k* that are found in the Old Testament. There are more than 400 with *b* and 250 with *k*. In Ugaritic the infinitive *construct* is used with *b* as a temporal clause, e. g., *bbk. krt* "as Keret wept." For other examples cf. Cyrus H. Gordon, *Ugaritic Handbook*, 1947, p. 68.

IV

THE EVIDENCE: Vocabulary

LEAVING THE REGION of what we call grammar, and coming into the sphere of rhetoric, we find that the critics of the Old Testament are in the habit of determining the date of documents and the sources and divisions and evolutions of literary works on the basis of diction, style, ideas, and aim. To this method no objection can justly be made, provided that we put the four items together and do not divorce them as is too often done. Besides, we must place them in the proper logical order of aim, ideas, style, and diction. For it is manifest that an author's aim or purpose in writing a given document will determine for him the ideas, reasons, and illustrations, which he uses to attain his purpose. It is no less evident that his style and diction will be influenced largely by the aim and ideas. In criticizing a literary work, therefore, the aim of the writer is to be considered first of all; then the ideas or reasons that he gives to reach his aim; and last, the method, style, and diction which he uses. When the author clearly announces his purpose as Thucydides does in his *History*, or Luke in his *Gospel*, or Milton in *Paradise Lost*, we are relieved of the labor of discovering this purpose for ourselves and are left free to discuss the method, reasons, and illustrations by which he attempts to fulfill his purpose; and also, the style, the diction and phraseology, which he employs.

This long excursus has been deemed necessary because in the literary criticism of the Old Testament the discussion has too often become confined to one or the other of the above points, instead of considering them all together; and especially because it is frequently argued that a difference of style and diction implies a difference of authorship and date, whereas it may imply simply a difference of aim and ideas. The diction and style of some of Milton's poems and letters and of his *Christian Doctrine* are so different from those of *Paradise Lost* and the *Areopagitica*, that, if his aim is left out of consideration, we might infer a difference of authorship. Walt Whitman and Longfellow differ so much in style that we might infer a different age. In doing so, we would be following the method of the destructive literary critics of the Old Testament. For, as we shall proceed to show, they often infer a difference of authorship or age, from a difference of diction or style, without due consideration of the fact that these differences may be due to difference of aim and ideas. In confirmation of this statement, attention is called to the long list of words and phrases given in LOT[1] to show that the Pentateuch was written by many different authors and at many different times; and to the lists[2] given to show that Jonah, Daniel, and Chronicles were written at a much later date than the apparent aim of the books would imply, or the ideas demand.

Before leaving generalities and coming to particulars, it may be well to make a few remarks about the aims and ideas of a literary work. *First,* as to aim, it must be kept in mind that an author may have a general aim including his

---

[1] Pp. 99-102, 131-135.
[2] LOT, 322, 506-7, 535-540.

whole work and a particular aim for each part of the general work; just as in an army the purpose of the whole is to defeat the enemy and the general staff makes out a plan of campaign and co-ordinates all the parts of the service to this end, while each branch of the service — infantry, artillery, airplane, engineers, and commissary — has its particular staff and purpose. Thus, the main purpose of Milton's works was to maintain the sovereignty of God and the liberty of man; "to justify the ways of God to man," and to defend "the liberty to know, to utter, and to argue freely, according to conscience."

So the purpose of the Old Testament is to teach the uniqueness, sovereignty, justice, and holiness of God, His gracious intention to redeem mankind, and the holiness of His people to be attained through faith and obedience, repentance, atonement, and love; and the aim of every part of the Old Testament is to subserve the purpose of the whole. Keeping this great purpose in view, we can see how every part of every book conduces to the purpose of the whole; and how the different ideas of the prophets and historians and poets and wise men, expressed in various styles and dictions, all illumine and concenter to the attainment of the one great end.

Second, let it be remembered that while the purpose of every part of a work should conduce to the purpose of the whole, it is not true that the special purpose of every part should be the same as that of every other part. *Paradise Lost* has a different purpose from the *Areopagitica; The Christian Doctrine* from *The State Papers;* the sonnets on the Waldenses and on his own blindness from those on Cromwell and on those

> That bawl for freedom in their senseless mood,
> And still revolt when truth would set them free.

So, also, in the books of Scripture, the purpose of the Psalter is to afford us a book of prayers and praises;[3] but each psalm has a special purpose of its own, and that purpose is attained by an appropriate array of ideas clothed in a suitable style and verbiage. Like the gardens of Versailles, the general plan is one, but the plans of the different beds are many and the gorgeous effect of the whole is produced by the harmonious arrangement of the various flowers, the mingling and blending of the colors, the contrasts of light and shadow, the long allées, the pendant branches of the trees, the fountains and statues, the palaces of man and the atmosphere and vaulted heavens and glaring sun.

Third, the ideas and reasons given to attain the end in view will be as varied as the imagination of the author can suggest. This seems so obvious that it will surprise some of our readers to know that critics actually allege against the genuineness of parts of the Bible that they contain new ideas and reveal a tone different from what we find elsewhere in the author's works. Thus: "modern critics agree generally in the opinion that this prophecy [i. e., Isa. 24-27] is not Isaiah's; and chiefly for the following reasons: (1) It lacks a suitable occasion in Isaiah's age" — a reason which means simply that the critics know of none. (2) "The literary treatment is in many respects unlike Isaiah's." (3) "There are features in the representation and contents of the prophecy which seem to spring out of a different (and later) vein of thought from Isaiah's."[4] So, also, Micah 6 and 7 are assigned to a different author from 1-5 because they are said to have "a different tone and manner," and because, as Kuenen remarks, "the author does not carry on, or develop lines of thought contained in 1-5.[5] Parts of Zephaniah are doubted because they are thought to express the ideas

---

[3] In the Mishna, the Psalter is called *tehillim,* "Praises" (cf. Ps. 72:20).

[4] LOT, 219, 220.

[5] *Idem* 333.

and hopes of a later age."[6] Several passages in Hosea are held to be a later addition because they are "thought to express ideas alien to Hosea's historical or theological position."[7] Now, these and all such opinions are absolutely worthless as evidence. In fact, they are not evidence at all in a legal or scientific sense; for they have in their favor no reasons resulting from investigations. For the 55 years of Manasseh in whose reign Ewald would place Micah 6 and 7 we have a record of but 18 verses. For the life and circumstances of Isaiah, we have but a few chapters in Kings. Of Hosea's life we know only what he tells us and of Zephaniah's we know nothing, except that he lived "in the days of Josiah the son of Ammon king of Judah."[8] And so for critics who deny even the additional information supplied by the Book of Chronicles and the reliability of the headings to express opinions as to what the prophets may have thought or as to what the events and circumstances of their lives may have been is simply absurd. It is not even as good as hearsay evidence. It is pure imaginings. The critic who puts such opinions forth as evidence is no better than a witness who would testify that an accused was guilty because of his race, or religion, or looks. It involves, also, on his part a presumptuousness, or self-conceit, which borders on megalomania, a disease from which Caesars and Kaisers do not alone suffer.

The reader will please pardon the indefiniteness of the above discussion. Witnesses we can cross-examine, documents we can investigate; but when a critic, or alleged expert, gives opinions based on opinions and not on reasons derived from experiments and investigation of objective facts, we can only have him ruled out of court, and request the judge to quash the indictment. Leaving, therefore, these

---

[6] *Idem* 342.

[7] *Idem* 306.

[8] Zeph. 1:1.

aerial heights of speculation, in which one man is as much of an expert as another, or in his own estimation a little better, let us come down to the objective, obvious facts of earth and let us consider and test the testimony of the documents involved in the words and phrases contained in them.

WORDS ALLEGED TO BE LATE

We are prepared to maintain that a large part of the words that are produced as evidence of the late date of documents containing them cannot themselves to be proved to be late. For, first, no one can maintain that because a word occurs only in a late document the word itself is therefore late;[9] for in this case, if a late document was the only survival of a once numerous body of literature, every word in it would be late; which is absurd. Nor, second, can one maintain that a document is late merely because it contains words which do not occur in earlier ones, which are known to us. Every new find of Egyptian Aramaic papyri gives us words not known before except, if at all, in documents written hundreds of years later. Nor, third, is a word to be considered as evidence of the lateness of a document in which it occurs simply because it occurs again in documents known to be late, such as the Hebrew parts of the Talmud. And yet, this is frequently affirmed by the critics. Thus LOT mentions about twenty of such words to prove that Daniel and Jonah are later by centuries than the times of which they treat.[10] In this Dr. Driver was simply following in the footsteps of the German scholars who preceded him. It may be considered a sufficient answer to such alleged proofs to affirm (what anyone with a Hebrew concordance can confirm for himself) that Daniel, Jonah, Joel, and the Psalter, and other

---

[9] See the discussion and proof of this statement in *Studies in the Book of Daniel*, p. 320f.

[10] LOT 322, 504-8.

documents of the Old Testament have no larger percentage of such words than those which the critics assign to an early date, and that Isaiah 24-27 and Psalm 139, which they consider to be among the latest parts of their respective books, are distinguished from most of the other parts of the Old Testament by having no such words at all. Finally, it is obvious that a kind of proof that will prove almost everything to be late, and especially the parts considered late to be early, is absurd and inadmissible as evidence in a case designed to prove that some documents are later than others because they contain words of this kind. For it is certain that if all are late, then none are early — a conclusion which would overthrow the position of all critics, radical as well as conservative; and since this conclusion is desired and maintained by none, it must be dismissed as *absurd*.

In proof, however, that such words are found in every book, and in almost every part of every book, of the Old Testament we subjoin the following tables. These tables are based on special concordances of every book and of every part of every book of the Old Testament, prepared by and now in the possession of the writer of this article. In accordance with the laws of evidence, that "witnesses must give evidence of facts," that "an expert may state general facts which are the result of scientific knowledge, and that an expert may give an account of experiments [hence, also, of investigations] performed by him for the purpose of forming his opinion,"[11] it may add force and clearness to the evidence about to be presented, if an account is first given of the way in which the facts upon which the tables are based were collected. One whole summer was spent in gathering from a Hebrew concordance all the words in the Old Testament that occur there five times or less, giving also the places where the words occur. A second summer

---

[11] Stephen, *The Law of Evidence*, pp. 100, 103, 112.

sufficed for making from this general concordance a special concordance for each book. In the third summer, special concordances were made for J, E, D, H, and P, for each of the five books of the Psalter and for each of the psalms; for each of the parts of Proverbs, and of the alleged parts of Isaiah, Micah, Zechariah, Chronicles, Ezra, Nehemiah; and for such parts as Genesis 14 and the poems contained in Genesis 49; Exodus 15; Deuteronomy 32; 33; and Judges 5. Then, each of the words of this kind was sought for in the Aramaic and in the Hebrew of the post-Biblical Jewish writers. The evidence of the facts collected is manifest, and we think, conclusive.

A study of these percentages should convince everyone that the presence of such words in a document is no proof of its relative lateness.[12]

	Number of words occurring in O. T. five times or less	Per-centage of these words in Talmud		Number of words occurring in O. T. five times or less	Per-centage of these words in Talmud
Psalm 79	3	00.0	Ezekiel	335	24.9
Proverbs 31:1-9	0	00.0	Lamentations	56	25.0
Isaiah 24-27	0	00.0	Haggai	4	25.0
Obadiah	7	14.3	Ezra 7-10	8	25.0
Isaiah 36-39	7	14.3	Zechariah 2	16	25.0
Judges-Ruth	107	15.8	Isaiah 40-66	62	25.8
Nahum	36	16.7	Proverbs 1-9	69	27.5
Ezra 1-6	6	16.7	Daniel	47	29.8
Micah 2	11	18.2	Zechariah 1	22	30.8
Isaiah 34-35	5	20.0	Zechariah 3	12	30.8
Isaiah 13-15	10	20.0	Micah 1	22	31.8
Isaiah (1st pt.)	121	22.3	Job	374	31.0
Malachi	13	23.1	Jeremiah	278	32.1

[12] In explanation of these tables it may be said that they are prepared with special reference to the critical analysis of the O. T. Thus the Pentateuch is arranged according to the documents, J, E, D, H, and P; and the Proverbs are divided into seven portions (following LOT). The first column of the tables gives for each book or part of a book the number of words occurring five times or less in the O. T. that are found in it; and the second column the percentage of these words that are to be found in the same sense in the Hebrew of the Talmud.

Psalms	514	33.1	Elohist (E)	119	48.7
Book I	123	35.8	Proverbs 31:10-31	6	50.0
Book II	135	31.1	Holiness Code		
Book III	76	30.3	(H)	48	50.0
Book IV	61	31.1	Chronicles	144	51.5
Book V	118	34.7	Proverbs 25-29	52	51.9
Micah 3	15	33.3	Esther	57	52.6
Proverbs 10-22:16	80	33.8	Priest Code (P)	192	53.1
Proverbs 22:17-24	30	36.7	Deuteronomist		
Samuel-Kings	356	37.2	(D)	154	53.2
Habakkuk	34	38.2	Proverbs 30	15	53.5
Joel	28	39.3	Song of Songs	99	54.6
Jonah	15	40.0	Nehemiah	48	56.3
Hosea	65	41.5	Ecclesiastes	77	57.1
Jehovist (J)	162	44.4	Memoirs of		
Zephaniah	31	45.2	Nehemiah	27	59.3
Amos	50	46.0			

A careful reading of this table will justify the statement made above that a "kind of proof that will prove almost everything to be late, and especially the parts considered late to be early, is absurd and inadmissible as evidence in a case designed to prove that some documents are later than others because they contain words of this kind." This kind of evidence would simply prove almost all the documents of the Old Testament to be late. If admitted as valid, it would militate as much against the views of the radicals as it would against those of the conservatives.

Take, for example, the number of these words occurring in the alleged documents of the Pentateuch. J and E together have 281 words in about 2,170 verses (one in less than every 7 7/10 verses) and about 46 per cent of these words are found in the Talmud; D has 154 words in about 1,000 verses (or one in every 6 5/10 verses) and about 53 per cent of them in the Talmud, and PH 201 words in 2,340 verses (or one in every 8 6/10 verses) and about 52 per cent of the words in the Talmud. Surely, no unbiased judge of literature would attempt to settle the dates of documents on such slight variations as these from one word in 6 5/10 to one in 8 6/10 and from 46 to 53 per cent in the Talmud! Besides, in regard to the relative proportion in verses the order is PH, JE, D in percentages in the Talmud JE, PH, D; but according to the Wellhausians, it should in both cases be JE, D, PH. The slight variations in both cases point to unity of authorship and likeness of date.

Take another example from Micah. Micah 1-3 was written, according to some critics, about 700 B.C.; 4 and 5 about 550 B.C.; and 6 and 7 about 650 B.C. Yet the first part has 22 words with about 32 per cent in the Talmud; the second part 11 words with 18 per cent in the Talmud; and the third part 15 words with 33 per cent in the Talmud. The latest part has the fewest words and the smallest per cent.

In the parts of Isaiah ascribed by the critics to Isaiah there are 121 words occurring five times or under in the Old Testament of which 22.3 per cent are found also in the Talmud; whereas, in the parts ascribed to the Exile or later there are 84 words of which 23.8 per cent are found in the Talmud. Chapters 24—27 have no such words, but are the latest of all according to most of the radical critics.

Chronicles has 144 of these words; but 68 occur in the parts not parallel with Kings, and 84 in the parallel parts. (The seeming discrepancy in the numbers here is because four of the words occur in both parts of Chronicles.) As there are about 950 verses in the original part and only about 700 verses in the parallel portions, it will be seen that in the original parts of Chronicles there is one of these words in about every fourteen verses and in the parallel parts in every eight.

It is incumbent in those who make use of this alleged evidence from New Hebrew words to show, also, how Malachi, the latest of the prophets, has only 23.1 per cent of words of this kind occurring in the Talmud; whereas, Hosea has 41.5 and Amos 46, Joel 39.3 and Jonah 40. Also, while they are at it, will they please show how Proverbs 30:1-9 has none of these words, although they all place it among the postexilic literature.

The extraordinary number of words occurring only in Ecclesiastes and the Song of Songs is no indication of date but rather of authorship and subject. Solomon being the wisest man of his time and a poet, an observer of nature and of man, would, like Shakespeare, Milton, and Carlyle, have a vocabulary much beyond the average. Besides, the subject of the Song of Songs is not treated elsewhere in the Old Testament and it is not fair to take the use of words in an idyll of bucolic love, such as ointment, washing, espousal, powder, kid, roe, and locks of hair, as an indication of date. And again the author of Ecclesiastes, as a philosopher, may well have indulged in abstract terms; and as a moralist who better than Solomon may have spoken of youth, and poverty and weariness and vanity!

Of the 16 words of this kind in the Memoirs of Nehemiah, six are found in works admitted by the critics to antedate 550 B.C., one is in New Aramaic but not in New Hebrew, four or five are Babylonian, three refer to the walls and buildings of Nehemiah, and one to the genealogies. The only one left is found in Daniel also. Thus we see that the apparently alarming number and percentage of *late* words even in Nehemiah reduces itself to a matter of subject. All the words suit the time and the man and his deeds.

The small number of these words in Ezra is one of the most noteworthy facts in evidence. Surely, a book written, as the critics allege, at about 300 B.C. (LOT 540 f.) should have had a large number of these words! But not one word is found in the two documents into which the critics divide the book. Out of the 14 words in Ezra found five times or less in the Old Testament, seven are certainly and two probably derived from the Persian or Babylonian, one (*'ashem* 10:19) is found also in E and II Samuel, and does not occur in New Hebrew; the root of *Yesud* is used in all ages of Hebrew literature and besides the argument depends on a vowel pointing, and again, the root is used in Babylonian; one *abeduth* 9:8,9 may be Aramaic, but Ezra wrote about half his book in the Aramaic of the fifth century; one *ra'ad* 10:9 is found in Daniel 10:11; and Psalm 104:12 and its derivatives in Exodus 15:15; Isaiah 33:14; Job 41:4; and Psalms 2:11; 48:7; 55:6; and the last *mahalaf* may be connected with the Assyrian word meaning an instrument of wood or stone (Muss-Arnolt p. 316) or with the word meaning garment or harness *(idem)*.

We conclude, therefore, that this appeal of the critics to New Hebrew as an evidence of lateness for certain documents of the Old Testament is unwarranted by the facts in evidence. Tested in the light of present-day dictionaries and concordances of the Hebrew and cognate languages, it shrinks into absurdity.

THE ALLEGED ARAMAISMS

Exception is to be taken to the way in which the critics use the presence of Aramaisms in a document as a proof of its age; and also to their habit of assuming that words are Aramaisms, without presenting any proof in favor of their assumption. Now, an Aramaism in a Hebrew document must be defined as an Aramaic word which the writer of the Hebrew document has used to denote a thing, or to express a thought, either because there was no Hebrew word that he could equally well employ, or because he was himself strongly under Aramaic influence, or because he wanted to show off his acquaintance with foreign tongues; just as recent English writers use *hinterland* in describing the part of Africa lying back of the coast, or as Mr. Rider Haggard uses *trek* and *laager* in his novels whose scene is in South Africa; or as Carlyle uses many German words and phrases in his writings and even copies the style of Jean Paul Friedrich Richter; or as the debaters in the British Parliament used to interlard their speeches, or Montaigne and the writers in the *Spectator* their essays, with Latin. With such analogies before them, it is easy to see how the commentators of the eighteenth century fell into the habit of calling every infrequent word in the Hebrew Bible, whose root and form are common in Aramaic, by the name of Aramaism. It was simply their naïve way of camouflaging their ignorance with the appearance of knowledge. If they had said merely that this word which occurs only here in the Hebrew of the Old Testament is found frequently in Aramaic, they would in most cases have been exactly right. But when they inferred that because it was frequent in Aramaic and infrequent in Hebrew it was of Aramaic origin and a loanword in Hebrew, they indulged in a *non-sequitur,* as we shall now attempt to show.

The Consonantal Changes. In the Semitic group of languages there are three great families, which may be designated as the Hebrew, the Arabic, and the Aramaic. In these great families the radical sounds, ', *ḥ, b, m, p, g, k, q, l, n,* and *r* are usually written uniformly with corresponding signs, i. e., Hebrew *b* corresponds to Arabic *b*, and both to Aramaic *b, and ḥ (ch), w,* and *y,* correspond commonly in Hebrew and Aramaic. In preformatives and sufformatives Hebrew *h* is ' in the others; and in sufformatives Hebrew *m* is *n*. In the other eight (or nine, counting *sin*) radical sounds, however, certain regular changes occur, and seem to differentiate the three families. These changes may be illustrated by the following table which is based upon a collection of all the roots in the Hebrew Old Testament containing one or more of these eight radicals and upon a comparison of their roots in Arabic and Aramaic. There are 721 such roots in Hebrew which have corresponding roots in both Arabic and Aramaic. The numbers to the right show how often each correspondence is found in the roots of the Old Testament Hebrew.[13]

Hebrew	Arabic	Aramaic	Number of Roots
d	d	d	100
d	d	ṭ	1
d	dh	d	10
ṭ	ṭ	ṭ	71
ṭ	ẓ	ṭ	2
ṭ	t	ṭ	2
t	t	t	42
ẕ	th	t	5 (?)
sh	th	t	18
sh	t	t	4
sh	š	sh	88
sh	sh	sh	5 or 6 (?)
sh	š	s	1
š	sh	s	29
š	s	s	5

Hebrew	Arabic	Aramaic	Number of Roots
s	sh	s	5
s	s	s	45
s	ṣ	s	7
ṣ	ṣ	ṣ	36
ṣ	ṣ	ʿ	1
ṣ	ṣ	z	1
ṣ	z	ṣ	3
ṣ	ḍ	ṣ	10
ṣ	ḍ	ʿ	11
ṣ	ṭ	ṭ	1
ṣ	ẓ	ṭ	9
z	z	z	54
z	dh	d	18
ʿ	ʿ	ʿ	110
ʿ	ġ	ʿ	26
ʿ	ṣ,ḍ	ʿ	0

These three families have obviously, according to the above table, certain laws of consonantal change resembling Grimm's law in the Indo-European languages. Thus, when a Hebrew root has the radical consonant *sh* (*š*) it is generally *š* in Arabic: and in this case should be *sh* in Aramaic. Sometimes, however, the Hebrew *sh* corresponds to an Arabic *th*; and in this case the Aramaic is *t*. A *t* in Hebrew would be represented by a *t* in Arabic and by a *t* in Aramaic. These three series of changes are all common or regular and no proof of *borrowing* can be derived from the consonants themselves where these series exist. If, however, we have *t* in Hebrew, *th* in Arabic and *t* in Aramaic, the Hebrew word would probably be derived from the Aramaic, since

[13] For the Hebrew and Aramaic s = ס, ‘ = ע, ṣ = צ, sh = שׁ. š = שׂ, For the Arabic, the English equivalents as given in Wright's *Arabic Grammar* have been used.

the Hebrew form should according to rule have *sh*. Or, if we had *sh* in Hebrew, *t* in Arabic and *t* in Aramaic, the Arabic has probably been derived from the Aramaic.

Observing, then, the exceptions to the regular changes, we find that there are four or five roots or words in the Old Testament Hebrew that may possibly have been derived from the Aramaic, to wit, *nadar*, "to vow," *athar*, "to abound," *tillel* "to cover" (Neh. 3:15), *beroth* (Cant. 1:17), and *medibath* (Lev. 26:26).[13a]

1. As far as *nadar*, "to vow," is concerned, the fact that its root and its derivative noun for "vow" are found in Isaiah twice, Proverbs three times, Judges four times, Samuel seven times, eleven times in Deuteronomy, and 64 times elsewhere in the Old Testament Hebrew shows that if this irregularity indicates an Aramaic origin, it indicates also that Aramaic words were taken over into Hebrew as early as the time of the composition of Proverbs, Isaiah, Deuteronomy, and the sources of Judges and Samuel.

2. *Athar*, "to abound," occurs only in Proverbs and one derivative in Jeremiah 33:6;[14] and Ezekiel 35:13.

3. *Tillel* which is found only in Nehemiah 3:15 is admitted to be to all appearances an Aramaism. Since, according to the critics, it is in the Memoirs of Nehemiah, it must have been used by the author as early as the fifth century B.C.[15]

4. *Beroth* for the more usual *birosh*, "fir tree," may not be an Aramaism, but a peculiarity of the Hebrew dialect

---

[13a] The root *ndr*, "to vow," occurs several times in Ugaritic.

[14] Prov. 27:6 is in the part of Proverbs which Dr. Driver considers to have been rightly reputed to have been ancient in Hezikiah's age. (LOT, p. 407.) Ezekiel 35 is put by Dr. Driver at about 586 B.C. (LOT, 291, 262), and Jeremiah 33 in 587 B.C. (LOT, 262).

[15] LOT, 542, 552. The root *tll* occurs in Ugaritic in the sense "to fall," "to give dew." It would seem that Nehemiah 3:15 is the earliest extant usage of the root in the sense "to cover over."

of North Israel, where, to quote Dr. Driver (LOT, 449), "there is reason to suppose that the language spoken differed dialectically from that of Judah," and "approximated to the neighboring dialect of Phoenicia."[16] [17]

5. As to the *medibath,* in Leviticus 26:16, it is the wont of the critics to assume that it is the Hiphil participle of a verb *dub* which occurs in Aramaic, as the equivalent of the Hebrew *zub,* "to flow."[17a] In our opinion, however, it is better to take it to be the Hiphil participle of *da'ab,* "to be weak," and for the following reasons:

a. *Zub* is used in Leviticus 20:24; 22:4; both passages as well as 26:16 belonging to what the critics call the Law of Holiness. The verb and its derivatives are found also in P 34 or more times, in Deuteronomy six times, in J in Exodus 3:8; 13:5; in E in Exodus 3:17; and in JE in Exodus 33:3. Why should the writers of H, or the various *later* redactors have used two methods of spelling?

b. *Zub* is used of the flowing of various issues and of milk and honey, but is never employed with *soul,* nor in any but a physical sense except perhaps in Lamentations 4:9; but even there it probably refers to the flowing of the blood of the slain.

c. None of the Aramaic versions, except possibly the

---

[16] The best discussions of the characteristics of the different Semitic families will be found in Wright's *Comparative Grammar of the Semitic Languages;* Zimmern, *Vergleichende Grammatik der Semitischen Sprachen;* Brockelmann, *Grammatik der Semitischen Sprachen;* and Driver, in an appendix to his work *On the Tenses in Hebrew.*

[17] Besides, it is possible there may have been two words of similar but different meaning in Hebrew, just as in the Babylonian *burašu* and *berutu.* If we take Jensen's meaning of "selected woods" for the latter the meaning of the last clause of Cant. 1:17, would be "our water troughs are selected woods."

[17a] It should be noted that a noun *db,* "stream," from a root *dwb,* appears in Ugaritic. Hence, even if this particular form, *mediboth,* were derived from *dub,* that would certainly be no evidence of lateness. The word *dabum* (to be consumed by ?) appears in the Mari tablets.

Syriac, render Leviticus 26:16 as if they considered the participle to come from a verb "to flow."[18]

d. *De'abon* in Deuteronomy 28:65 is rendered by Onkelos and Jonathan as well as in the Samaritan and Syriac by words showing that the Hebrew scholars who made these versions considered the Hebrew word in Deuteronomy 28:65 to have the same root as the word in Leviticus 26:16.[19]

e. *Da'ab* in Jeremiah 31:12,25 is rendered in the Targum by *yeṣof*, "to be vexed," and a derivative in Job 41:14 by *de'abon*.

f. The Aramaic of the Talmud confuses the two verbs *dub* and *de'ab*.[20]

g. The Aleph is frequently omitted in the Hebrew and Aramaic forms and manuscripts.[21]

For these reasons we feel justified in refusing to admit that the *mediboth* of Leviticus 26:16 can be used as proof that there is an Aramaism in H.[22] The critics are at liberty to make the most out of the presence of *ṭillel*, "to cover,"[23] in the memoirs of Nehemiah (Neh. 3:15), which was written at a time when the Jews of Elephantine, Samaria, Jerusalem, Susa, and Ecbatana, all used the Aramaic as the language of business and correspondence. The wonder is that there should be only one sure instance of an Aramaism

---

[18] Onkelos has מפחת, Jonathan מסייפא, the Samaritan מדביאן, the Peshitto מדיבא. In this word which is of infrequent occurrence in Syriac, it is probably that the א has been changed to י. Compare Nöldeke's *Syriac Grammar*, § 33B.

[19] Onkelos and Jonathan have the same as Onkelos in Lev. 26:15; Samaritan has דכאות| or דזון and Syriac has דויבא.

[20] Dalman, *Aram.-Neu-Heb. Wörterbuch*, p. 84.

[21] Nöldeke, *Syriac Grammar*, 32, 33, 35; Gesenius, *Hebrew Grammar*, § 7 g; Siegfried, *Lehrbuch der neuheb. Sprache*, § 14; Wright, *Comparative Grammar*, pp. 44-47.

[22] ZATW. I., 177-276.

[23] P. 115.

in the Hebrew Bible, to be proved by the variations of the consonants out of a total of 721 possibilities.[24]

The Noun Formations. But not only in the region of consonantal changes does the attempt of the critics to prove their theories as to Aramaisms utterly break down, when a scientific investigation of the alleged evidence is made; it fails as certainly in the attempt to prove them by an appeal to the evidence of the *forms* of the words. We have already said that the noun forms ending in n[25] are found in all of the Semitic languages at all stages of their development and that the forms ending with *ûth* are numerous in Assyrian and Hebrew as well as in Aramaic.[26] The forms in *ûth* have already been sufficiently discussed above.[27]

The Nouns in *ôn* and *ân.* As to the forms in *n*, the following remarks may be added to what has been said.[28] Exclusive of proper names, about 140 nouns ending in *n* are found in Biblical Hebrew.[29] Sixty-three of these are met with in the Pentateuch. Of the 63, the Targum of Onkelos renders 12 by the same nouns ending in *n*, and 51 by other nouns, most of them not ending in *n*. Onkelos, however, contains 63 nouns ending in *n*. It will thus be seen that where the subject matter is exactly the same, the Hebrew original and the Aramaic version have exactly the same number of words ending in *n*. Judging from this fact, it is left to our

---

[24] Out of the 352 words treated of in Kautzch's *Die Aramäismen im Alten Testament,* ברות and טלל are the only ones that can be proved by the phonetic test.

[25] See Page 91.

[26] See Page 88.

[27] See Pages 88-91.

[28] See Page 91.

[29] The lists of Thotmes III have seventeen nouns ending in *n* out of 119 all told. The Sendscherli Inscriptions have no nouns in *n* but the Sachau papyri have scores. They are found also in the Sabaean and Minean Inscriptions and are common in Arabic and Syriac. There are 14 in the code of Hammurabi alone and 26 in Babylonian of the Amarna Letters.

readers to determine, if they can, whether the ending *n* is more characteristic of Aramaic than of Hebrew.

Again, in the case of the 12 words out of the 63 where they agree, is it more likely that the original Hebrew borrowed from, or was influenced by the Aramaic version, or *vice versa*, especially in view of the fact that according to the critics themselves, the version was not written for from 500 to 1,000 years after the original?

As might be inferred from the example of the usage of words with the ending *n* in the Pentateuch, it will be found that in the best specimens of Aramaic literature the number of nouns with this ending varies with the kind of literature. Thus in *Joshua the Stylite,* we find that in the first four chapters, where the dedication occurs, there are 19 words of this kind; whereas in certain chapters of the purely narrative parts, such as 19, 64, and 65, no word with this ending is found, and even long chapters like 21 and 22 have but one each, and 23 and 66 but three each. In Bar Hebraeus, also, we find two nouns of this kind in the narrative of the crusaders' first conquest of Jerusalem, one of them a word similar to one found in the Hebrew glosses of the Tel-el-Amarna Letters.[30]

Notwithstanding these general considerations and this common use of nouns with the ending *n* in Hebrew documents, the critics are wont to argue that certain parts of the Old Testament are late because they contain nouns of this kind. The most glaring example of the argument is that the presence of a number of such words in Ecclesiastes is due to Aramaic influence, the assumptions being made that many of the words in Ecclesiastes with this ending are Aramaisms, and that the mere use of Aramaisms indicates

---

[30] I.e., אחרון. Cp *aḥruna* in the letter of Biridiya to the King of Egypt (Winckler, 196, line 10).

a late date. In answer to these assumptions three statements of fact and evidence may be made.

1.   In general, it may be said that the number of different words of this kind in Ecclesiastes is small compared with what we find in Aramaic documents of a like character. For in 12 chapters, or 10 pages, of Ecclesiastes, there are but 17 words all told of this class, whereas in the first four pages of *Joshua the Stylite* there are 19. Yet in the 10 pages of *Joshua the Stylite* from 63 to 73 inclusive, there are but 12 as against 34 in the first 10 pages, showing that the number of such words varies in Aramaic as well as in Hebrew in accordance with the subject treated. It seems clear that the relatively large number of these words ending in *n* in Ecclesiastes as compared with other Old Testament books is due to the character of the subject matter rather than to the lateness of the time of composition. Further, it is a noteworthy fact, not mentioned by the critics, that of the 140 words in the Old Testament ending in *n*, only 26 are found in Syriac. Of these 26, six are said in Brockelmann's *Lexicon* to have been derived by the Syrians from the Hebrew, and eight more are found in either Babylonian or Arabic, or both; thus reducing to 12 the number of words which could possibly be derived by the Hebrews from the Syriac. But—

2.   Of the 12 words remaining, seven occur in Ecclesiastes. As to these, the following facts rule out the supposition that the Hebrew could have derived them from the Aramaic:

a.   Not one of them is found in any Aramaic document written before A.D. 200. The latest date given by any critic for Ecclesiastes is about 100 B.C.

b.   Since the Aramaic literature in which any of the words occur was written by Jews who had adopted Aramaic, it is more reasonable to suppose that the Jewish writers of Aramaic documents borrowed from their own literary and native language, than that early Hebrew writers borrowed from the Aramaic. At least, there is no evidence that these words existed in early Aramaic.[31]

c. The forms of *yuthron* and *husron* have a *u* in the first syllable in Aramaic and an *i* in Hebrew.

d. Shilton, it is true, is found only in Ecclesiastes 8:4,8; but its root occurs in Babylonian as well as in Hebrew and Arabic, and the form occurs in Arabic as well as Syriac.

e. Ḳinyân is found in Onkelos and Syriac; but in Hebrew it occurs in Proverbs 4:7 in a passage which the critics put among the earliest parts of the Old Testament. Besides, to call it late in the Hebrew language, we would have to prove that Genesis 31:18; 34:23; 36:6; Leviticus 22:11; Joshua 14:4; and Ezekiel 38:12,13, where it occurs also, are late.

f. Ra'yôn is found only in Ecclesiastes 1:17; 2:22; 4:16, but it is singular that, if it meant the same here as in Aramaic, the Syriac version should render it by *ṣibyan* in 2:22 and by *ṭurofo* in 1:17; and 4:16, and the Aramaic Targum in all these cases by *tebiruth.*

The corresponding word in Syriac is rendered by Brockelmann by *cogitatio, fictio, consilium,* and *voluntas;* in Dalman by *Gesinnung, Gedanke.* Must the writer of Ecclesiastes have borrowed the Aramaic form and have given it a different meaning? Why not rather suppose that he found the word already in Hebrew, formed regularly from the good old Hebrew root *ra'a* as *pidyon* from *pada* and *ga'yon* from *ga'a?*

g. Finally *kiśrôn* is the worst specimen of evidence of all. To be sure, it happens that in the Hebrew of the Old Testa-

---

[31] This Jewish Aramaic literature to which the critics appeal was written from A.D. 200 to 700. Of course, these words may have existed in Aramaic a thousand or more years before they were written in any document we now possess; but in like manner, they may have existed in Hebrew 1,000 years before they were written in any document now known.

ment it is used in Ecclesiastes alone; but how it can be said to have been derived by the writer from the Aramaic passes belief when we observe that the word has not been found in any Aramaic document of any dialect or time.[32]

3. Even if it could be proved that certain words in a Hebrew document had been derived from the Aramaic, it would not determine the date of the Hebrew document; because the latest evidence from the extra-Biblical inscriptions, as well as the Old Testament itself, goes to show that the Hebrews and Arameans were closely associated from a time long precedent to that at which the critics claim that the oldest documents of the Old Testament were written.[33]

THE MEANINGS OF WORDS

Finally, when we leave the region of sounds and forms and enter that of sense and meaning, we find that here also the critics make assertions with regard to the derivation and borrowing of words which are demonstrably contrary to the facts. In cases such as טלל (*tillel*, "covered," Neh. 3:15), it is easy to show the probability that the word is an Aramaism, because the proper letter for the first radical should have been *s*, not *t*, if the word had the probable original Hebrew form of writing and sound. In cases such as *hithhabberuth* (Dan. 11:23), it is easy to suppose an Aramaism, because the form is common in Aramaic and is met with but once besides in the Old Testament Hebrew. But when we come to words which have no indication *(indicia)* either in sound or form that they are of Aramaic

---

[32] On the other hand, the form *ku-šir* in the sense of "success" is found in Babylonian of the time of Abraham. (See Dennefeld's *Babylonisch-Assyrische Geburts-Omina*.) The root is not found in Aramaic till A.D. 137.

[33] Thus the *Aḥlamu*, a tribe of Arameans, are mentioned in one of the Amarna Letters (Winckler, 291, lines 6, 8); and Naharina, the Aramaic form of Naharayim, occurs in Egyptian as early as the time of Thotmes I. (Breasted, *Ancient Records*, II, 81.) See my article in the April number of the PTR for 1925.

origin, we often find the critics simply asserting as a fact that a word is an Aramaism without producing any proofs whatever to support the assertion.

Thus DeWette-Schrader[34] speak of *pashar, batal, tanaf,* and *kotel* as Aramaic, and a proof of the late date of Ecclesiastes and of the Song of Songs. They give no proof except the fact that the words are found in Aramaic. The evidence from this fact is nullified by the discovery that all four words are found in Babylonian, and all but the last one, in Arabic with exactly the same sound, form, and meaning which is characteristic of the Hebrew.

Again, Dr. Driver in LOT mentions among the words in Ecclesiastes and the Song of Songs "having usually affinities with the Aramaic nine that are"[35] found with appropriate sound, form, and meaning, in the Babylonian language and in documents long antedating the time of the captivity. Of these words, *sha* is not found in any pure Aramaic dialect, is the ordinary relative in Babylonian from the earliest to the latest documents, and is found in all periods of Hebrew literature;[36] and *'umman* (master-workman) and *shalheveth* (flame) are so distinctively Babylonian in form and sense that there can be no doubt that Aramaic as well as Hebrew derived them from the Babylonian.

Cornill *(Introduction to the Canonical Books of the Old Testament,* 449) calls (1) *badal,* (2) *'bâd,*[36a] (3) *zemân,* (4) *pithgâm,* (5) *ra'yôn,* (6) *gumâts,* and (7) *takkîf* purely Aramaic. The first of these is found in Babylonian and Arabic as well as in Hebrew and Aramaic. The classing of the second as an Aramaism depends upon the pointing. The Targum gave it the pointing of the word for slave or work-

---

[34] *Einleitung,* pp. 543, 561.

[35] *Op. cit.,* pp. 440, 474.

[36] See my article on הזהיר in PTR for 1919.

[36a] In Ugaritic the root 'bd means "to serve." and 'bd is a slave or servant.

man and renders by "their scholars who were subject to them." The third is found in Arabic in the verb forms as well as in many derivatives; whereas in Syriac there is no verb form and the nouns all have *b* instead of *m*. The fourth word is probably Hittite or Armenian; the fifth is not found in any Aramaic dialect in the sense it has in Ecclesiastes; and the sixth is not found in Syriac till the third century and then only in the Bible and in commentaries on the Bible. Besides, the usual form in Syriac has an *Ayin* for the third radical, showing that the form with *Tsadhe* was most probably derived from the Hebrew.

We leave it to our readers to decide whether it is more probable that the Hebrews derived these, and all such, words from the Babylonian (if indeed most of them are not primitive Semitic) documents, which at least antedated the Hebrew documents, rather than from the Aramaic, whose earliest use of the words so far as shown in writing, is in general from 300 to 1,000 years later than the time of the compilation of the Hebrew, even if with the critics we put Ecclesiastes as late as 100 B.C.

Finally, the late Prof. Kautzsch in his work on *Aramaisms in the Old Testament (Die Aramaismen im Alten Testamente)* gives about 350 words as being certainly, probably, or possibly, of Aramaic origin. Of these about 150 do not occur in form and sense in any Aramaic dialect. Two hundred and thirty-five are found in Hebrew or Hebrew and New Hebrew alone or in Hebrew and Babylonian, Arabic, or Ethiopic, or Phoenician. Only about 115 of the words, or roots, are found in Aramaic documents antedating the second century A.D., and only about 40 of these are not found in Babylonian, Arabic, Phoenician, or Ethiopic. Of the 350 words, the roots of about 25 are found in Phoenician or

Punic; of 17, in Sabean and Minean; of 50, in Ethiopic; of 150, in Arabic; and of more than 100 in Babylonian.

Of these 350 words 50 are found in the Pentateuch. If these 50 were really Aramaic words, we would expect the Aramaic versions to render them by some form from the same root. We find, however, that the Samaritan renders only 23 in this manner; the version of Onkelos 24; the Pseudo-Jonathan 14, and the Syriac Peshitto 17. That is, the translators of the Pentateuch from Hebrew into Aramaic, all of them excellent scholars, as their work shows, and all of them thoroughly acquainted with Hebrew and Aramaic, thought it necessary to translate from one-half to two-thirds of these 50 words in order to render them intelligible to the Aramaean readers! Besides the majority of the words rendered by words from the same root are found to have the same roots in Arabic, Ethiopic, or Babylonian. For example, the roots of 16 out of 24 such words in Onkelos are found also in Babylonian or Arabic.

Finally, of these 350 words, only 115 are found in Biblical Aramaic, together with the Aramaic inscriptions and papyri preceding 200 b.c.; and 80 of these 115 are found in root or form in Arabic or Babylonian. Of the remaining 235 words not more than 15 occur in any or all Aramaic documents antedating the time when the Peshitto Syriac version was made; that is, about a.d. 200.

In conclusion, then, it is evident that of these 350 words, about 100 have not been found in any Aramaic document, and that, according to the dates affixed to the Old Testament documents by the critics themselves, about 120 more of these words were used by the writers of the Old Testament from 350 to 700 years earlier than they have been found in any Aramaic document. We can easily understand how these translators of the Bible into the Aramaic dialects should have borrowed many words from the original, and how the Jews who wrote in Aramaic should have employed many Hebraisms; but how writers can have borrowed words from documents written 700 years after they were dead is a mystery for the critics to explain. If it is said that these Aramaic words may have existed and have been known to the Hebrew critics 700 years before they were written in Aramaic documents, we reply: so also can they have existed and have been known in Hebrew 700 years before they are found in Hebrew documents. Let us stick to the written documents. Assertion and conjecture are not evidence. And yet, it is on such alleged evidence as these so-called Aramaisms that the critics conclude that about 1,500 verses of the Old Testament, and often the sections and books in which they occur, must have been written after the Exile, or even after the time of Nehemiah. To the law and to the testimony, if they speak not according to this word it is because there is no light in them.[37]

THE USE OF SYNONYMS

We object to the assumption that the prevalent use of one synonym in one document and of another synonym in a second document is proof of difference of age or authorship.[38] A fine discrimination in the use of synonymous expressions is a proof rather of the superior rhetorical ability of one author than of an indiscriminate use of words by many authors. Yet the critics indulge themselves in elaborate collections of synonymous terms which they put forth as indisputable proof of difference of author and date.

Thus, *pada,* "to redeem," is said to be used by D in the same sense as *ga'al* by P. A closer study reveals the fact that in Babylonian, Arabic, and Aramaic, as well as in Hebrew,

---

[37] For a detailed treatment of Aramaisms in the Old Testament, see my articles in the *Presbyterian Review* for 1925.

[38] See my note on מנה (mana) and its synonyms in PTR for 1918.

the first of these verbs is used primarily and predominantly for the redemption from captivity; whereas *ga'al* is a verb found only in Hebrew and used specifically to describe certain duties of the next of kin, such as vengeance for blood, marrying the widow of a deceased kinsman, and others, including also the redemption from captivity. In some passages of the Pentateuch, as well as of the prophets, it is difficult for *us* to see why one should be used rather than the other; but generally it may be said that the next of kin (*gô'ēl*) performs his duty toward his captive kinsman (*gā'ûl*) by buying him back (פדה), i. e., paying the ransom money. Either verb might rightly be used, therefore, in speaking of the redemption. Any author of any age might have used either verb to denote this act of redeeming on the part of a kinsman, and there is no passage in the Pentateuch where either verb is used which could not as well have been written by the same author as all the other passages containing either.

DISTINCTIONS IN USAGE

We object to a word being considered as an evidence of age when no other word in the language could have expressed the exact meaning as well as the one employed. Thus *gîl* in Daniel 1:10 is said to indicate a date in the second century B.C. rather than the sixth. The only reason for this given in LOT[39] is that in the use of this word the Hebrew of Daniel resembles the Hebrew "of the age *subsequent to Nehemiah*," since it is used "also in Samaritan and Talmudic." We have already shown[40] that such resemblances for *hapax legomena* are found in every book of the Old Testament and not specifically in Daniel. It might be asked, also, why if it characterizes the age subsequent to Nehemiah, it is not found in Ecclesiasticus or the Zadokite

[39] P. 506, 10.
[40] P. 131 f.

Fragments. Or, if we press the argument, why then does it not prove that Daniel was written after the Zadokite Fragments, i. e., after A.D. 40? Of course, the critics will say that the writers of these books had no occasion to use the word, since they do not refer to any such band, or company of men as Daniel and his three companions. And they are right; but the same is true of all the writers of the other Old Testament books, and Daniel shows his linguistic ability in that to express a new idea, or a conception different from that employed by others, he has made use of a different word. For, we would like to ask the critics, what word is there in Hebrew that would so well convey the exact thought represented by *gîl*? The words for generation[41] would hardly suit, nor would the ordinary words for band or company.[42] For the author means to say just what he does say, that Daniel and his companions were brought up, or reared, with other youths of about the same age. Of course, they were of the same generation and perhaps of the same race and company and station in society, but the particular statement in Daniel 1:10 is that they were of about the same number of years of age. How else could the critics have said it better and more clearly? And how do we know that Moses, or David, or Isaiah, or Jeremiah would not have used the same word, if *they* had wanted to express the same idea? Let the critics tell us how *they* would have done it, if they had been writing in the sixth century B.C. Let them cease to cite the traditional authority *(sic!)* of DeWette-Schrader and other scholars and think out some way of bettering this "rotten" *(verderbte)* Hebrew.[43] As an interested onlooker,

---

[41] תולדה and דור.

[42] חבל in I Sam. 10:5,10, used of the company of prophets and in Ps. 119:61 of the wicked; or חבר as used in Hosea 6:9 of the priests, are the best possible words. But these could not be translated by *age*, in such phrases as "about your age."

[43] *Der verderbte Charakter des Idiomes in den hebraisch concipirten Abschnitten* is cited by De Wette-Schrader (*Einleitung*, p. 499) in favor of the late date of Daniel.

we expect to see them confounded in all their attempts to beat Daniel at writing Hebrew. In fact, with all his difficult passages, we think him excellent — much better, in fact, than anything in the Hebrew line of literature that either his German or English detractors can themselves produce.

OTHER PECULIARITIES OF STYLE OR DICTION

We object to considering a word or phrase recurrent in one document as being in itself a proof of a particular age. Kipling's "that is another story" might have been written any time in the last 500 years. So "I am Jehovah" might have been written at any time from Abraham to Christ.

Nor is the fact that certain words occur in one document and certain other words in another to be taken as constituting proof of different authors for the two documents. Milton uses scores of words in his *Areopagitica* which are never found in any of his poetical works. He employs hundreds of words and phrases in some of his works that are not found in others of his works.[44] Why may Moses and Isaiah not have done the same? The fact of the variations of words and idioms is one thing, the reasons for the variations are another thing. That certain words for "create" and "make" are used in Genesis 1 and certain others in Genesis 2 is a fact; but if this proves different authors, how about the 32 words which are found in the Koran to express the same idea? Are we to conjure up a dozen or more authors of the Koran to account for the variations in the vocabulary? We promise as Christians to nurture or train our children; but we speak of rearing, raising, educating, teaching, or bring-

---

[44] Thus on pages 94-97 of *The Aeropagitica* (Bohn's edition of the Prose Works of Milton, Vol. II) he uses 73 words not found at all in his poetical works. There are 584 *hapax legomena* in Milton's poetical works beginning with the letter *a* alone. See the *Lexicon to the English Poetical Works of John Milton*, by Laura E. Lockwood, Ph.D., a work much to be commended for study to those who would engage in the Higher Criticism of the Old Testament.

ing them up. In some churches they "take up a collection"; in others, they "make an offering." Differences of word and idiom are not so much indications of difference in age and author as they are of difference in subject matter, fecundity of conception, and fertility of expression.[45] One great writer will use a larger vocabulary and more idioms than twenty men with small knowledge and less language.

CONCLUSION

In conclusion, we claim that the assaults upon the integrity and trustworthiness of the Old Testament along the line of language have utterly failed. The critics have not succeeded in a single line of attack in showing that the diction and style of any part of the Old Testament are not in harmony with the ideas and aims of writers who lived at, or near, the time when the events occurred that are recorded in the various documents. In every case, it seems clear that the language suits the age at which the prima-facie evidence of the document indicates that it was written. We boldly challenge these Goliaths of ex-cathedra theories to come down into the field of ordinary concordances, dictionaries, and literature, and fight a fight to the finish on the level ground of the facts and the evidence.

---

[45] See my article on *The Authenticity of Jonah* in PTR for 1918.

V

THE EVIDENCE: History

FINALLY, let us review the framework of Old Testament history as a whole and see how it stands the tests which modern scientific research has brought to bear upon it. Can a man of scientific attainments still place any reliance upon the chronological, geographical, and other historical statements of the books of the Old Testament canon? Or has the light from Egypt and Babylon dispelled as a baseless fabric of a vision of the night that which was formerly considered to be a real structure of historic fact?[1a]

THE CHRONOLOGY

Let us look at the chronology of the Bible, beginning with the time of Abraham.

1. In the four great systems of Biblical chronology prepared from the Biblical statements alone, before anything definite was known in the fields of Egyptian and Babylonian archaeology, Hales puts the time of Abram's leaving Haran at 2078 B.C., Jackson at 2023, Petavius at 1961, and Ussher at 1921. Since Genesis 14 places Abraham in the time of Hammurabi, it is fair to ask when the Assyriologists date

---

[1a] See Appendix 2 e.

the reign of the latter. Jeremias puts him at about 2000 B.C.,[1] Clay at about 2100 B.C.[2] It will thus be seen that the date of Abraham as deduced from the facts provided by the Biblical text alone has been confirmed in a wonderful way by the evidence derived from Babylonian sources.

2. The relative date of Shishak, king of Egypt, corresponds to that of Rehoboam and is certainly to be placed somewhere in the tenth century B.C.[3]

3. The relative dates of the kings of Israel and Judah between the division of the kingdom and the fall of Samaria, as given in the Bible, correspond in general with what we find on the Assyrian monuments.

4. The relative dates of the kings of Assyria and Egypt as given on the monuments of their respective countries correspond with what we find in the Old Testament books.

5. The relative dates of the Babylonian kings Nebuchadnezzar, Evil-merodach, and Belshazzar agree in Biblical and monumental accounts. The order is correct in whatever sense Belshazzar may have been king.

6. The relative dates of the Cyrus of Ezra, the Darius of Haggai and Zechariah, and the Xerxes and Artaxerxes of Ezra are certainly correct; notwithstanding the difficulties in explaining the passage in Ezra 4.

It is thus apparent that the general scheme of chronology which underlies the history recorded in the Old Testament is abundantly justified by the evidence disclosed by the extra-Biblical records of antiquity. As to the apparently conflicting statements of the present Hebrew text, it must be remembered that many of them are doubtless occasioned by the inevitable corruptions in the text, arising from the prac-

---

[1] *The Old Testament in the Light of the Ancient East*, I, 322. It is now clear that Gen. 14 does not place Abraham in the time of Hammurabi. Hammurabi is currently dated about 1700. (See note 12, p. 65.)

[2] *Light on the Old Testament from Babel*, 130.

[3] See Jeremias, *op. cit.* II, 204 f.

tical impossibility of transcribing numerical data with accuracy. No one knows how numbers were denoted in the original Hebrew documents. It is known that the Egyptians, Babylonians, Phoenicians, Arameans, Nabateans and Palmyrenes, denoted numbers by a system of notation signs. The earliest example of the use of a letter of the alphabet in a Semitic document to denote a number is in the Egypto-Aramaic inscriptions where *b* seems to be used for *two* and *ṭ* for *nine*.[4] A double system of numerical signs and letters seems to have existed among the Syrians till the ninth century A.D.[5] Sometimes the signs were given and the number written also in full as in the Sendschirli [Senjirli] inscriptions.[6] In the Mesha and Siloah inscriptions the numbers are written in full.[7] In the Sachau papyri they are commonly denoted by signs.

A comparison of the Aramaic recension of the Behistun inscription with the Babylonian shows numerous variations in the numerical statements. Since these variations can hardly have been intentional, they show how easy it was to originate variations in manuscripts when there was no special purpose in being accurate. It made little difference to anyone whether the army of Darius killed or took alive a few more or less in a given battle. And certainly, these variations afford no proof of late date or of lack of genuineness or authenticity on the part of the various recensions of Darius' great inscription.

So, also, with the variations in the texts and manuscripts of the Old Testament, we must not exaggerate the importance of the difference in numerical statements, as if such difference argued in general against the veracity or genuineness of the original documents. In view of the

---

[4] Sachau, *Aramaische Papyrus u. Ostraka*, p. 276, and Sayce-Cowley *in loco*.
[5] Sachau, *idem*.
[6] Lidzbarski, *Nordsemitische Epigraphik*, p. 198.
[7] *Idem*.

numerous variations in the contemporaneous, or almost contemporaneous, recensions of the Behistun inscription, we
should rather be astonished that the numerical statements
of the Old Testament have been handed down with such
marvelous comparative accuracy, as that we can reconstruct
from the chronological data a framework of chronology
which harmonizes so closely with that revealed by the monuments.[7a]

THE GEOGRAPHY

The geographical statements of the Old Testament are
also marvelously in harmony with the evidence presented
by the documents of Egypt and Babylon.

1.   Thus the names of nations and cities mentioned in
the history of Abraham are in general such as are known
from the inscriptions to have been existent at the time of
Hammurabi,[8] or such as may have existed in his time,[9] or
whose existence in his time cannot be denied on the ground
of any evidence we possess,[10] or such as may well have been
substituted for older names in order to make the narra-
tion intelligible to the readers of later times.[11] This last
alternative, which affords the only real or supposed difficulty with regard to the possibility of the historical character
of the narrative, would be obviated if we suppose that the
account of Abraham's life was originally written in cuneiform; because in that system of writing the signs might be
read in different ways. For example, the name of the city
of Babylon was written in Sumerian *Ka-dingir-ra-ki* or *E-ki*,
or *Din-tir-ki*, or it was written in Babylonian as *maḫazu
Ba-bi-li*. In all four cases the Babylonian scribes of the time

---

[7a] An excellent discussion of Hebrew chronology is to be found in Edwin
R. Thiele, *The Mysterious Numbers of the Hebrew Kings*, Chicago, 1951.

[8] Such as Egypt, Elam, Larsa, Babylon, and Ur.

[9] Such as Harran, Damaskus, and Beer-sheba.

[10] Such as Hebron.

[11] Such as Dan and Philistia.

of Nebuchadnezzar and Cyrus must have pronounced the name as *Babili,* though an ignorant reader might have spelled out the three first groups of signs as *Ka-dingir-ra-ki* or *E-ki* or *Din-tir-ki* respectively, these being doubtless the earlier designations of the place in Sumerian, before the Semitic conquerors appeared on the scene. So Laish may have been written with the signs *la* and *ish* in cuneiform and might be read as Laish, or after the conquest by the Danites as Dan.[12] As for *Pelishtim* (Philistines), we may compare the Sumerian *nim-ma-ki,* the equivalent in the Babylonian recension of the Behistun inscription of the Persian *uvaga* and of the Susian *haltamti* (or *hutamti*) and of the more usual Babylonian *E-lam-mat.*[13] Weissbach correctly transliterates the Sumerian signs *nim-ma* by the Babylonian word *elamtu.* So the signs rendered by *Pelishtim* in our Hebrew Bibles may originally have denoted another name. That is, the sign for the land or city often remained the same, but the denotation of the signs changed. The examples of this in the cuneiform documents are so numerous that, if it could be proved that the names Dan and Pelishtim did not exist in the time of Abraham, we would be amply justified in supposing that in the documents written in that time they were denoted by signs that could afterward be properly read by the Hebrews in two different ways.

2. That the names of cities and nations mentioned in Genesis 10 suit the time of Moses better than any other time was fully discussed in an article of the present writer in the *Presbyterian and Reformed Review* for 1884. If we add to what was then written the fact of the probable double reading of the cuneiform signs in certain cases, the conclusions of that article will be corroborated and no reasonable doubt can longer be entertained that the genealogies of

[12] The same Chinese sign is read Seoul in Korean and Heijo in Japanese. Another sign is read Pyongyang in Korean and Heijo in Japanese.
[13] See Weissbach, *Die Keilenschriften der Achaemeniden,* p. 143.

Genesis 10 harmonize with the state of geographical science in the time of Ramses II. This well-known method of double reading might explain also such difficult words as *Casluhim* and *Napthtuhim*[14] — words that have hitherto baffled the interpreters of all schools at whatever time they place the date of the composition of Genesis 10.

3. The discovery of Pithom and Rameses[15] has established forever the firm foundation of the account of the Exodus.[16]

4. The appropriate manner, both as to time and place, with which the proper names of cities and countries are used in the Old Testament defies all hostile criticism directed against the genuineness of the narratives. The marvelous way in which such countries, nations, and cities as Elam, the Hittites, the old Babylonians, the Assyrians, the Egyptians and Ethiopians, the Moabites, and the Edomites; Tyre, Sidon, Damascus, Hamath, Separad, and scores of other names of places, are brought into the Biblical narrative, each in its proper place and time, and generally with the very spelling as accurate as could be expected, is beyond comparison in any ancient document. In view of the fact that the Biblical records have stood the test of extra-Biblical evidence in scores of cases where its testimony is clear and indisputable, it is inadmissible to claim that the Biblical documents are wrong, either when there is no evidence on the monuments,[17] or whenever we with our limited knowledge of the facts and circumstances cannot explain satisfactorily the location and collocation of the name.[18]

---

[14] Knight in *The Nile and the Jordan* (pp. 168, 169) identifies *Casluhim* with the *Kasluhit* of the Kom Ombo list.

[15] See Naville: *The Store-City of Pithom and the Route of the Exodus.* Egypt. Expl. Fund, 1885 (4th Ed., 1903) and *Goshen*, 1887.

[16] See Naville, *The Store Cities of the Exodus.*

[17] As in the case of the Hivites, Girgashites, Magog, etc.

[18] As in the case of Tiras, Ashkenaz, Sabtah, and a few other names in Gen. 10.

5. Another fact that must always be kept in mind in discussing the Old Testament is this: It was from the beginning according to its own testimony meant to be a book for the people and not for antiquarians and scholars merely.[19] Hence, we can well believe that as the designation of certain places changed, the text of the Bible was often changed accordingly. This would account for such possible changes as *Dan* and *Pelishtim*; just as we might and do speak of Constantinople[19a] as having been from the time of the glory of Greece the busy center of commercial activity and of New York Bay as having been entered by Henry Hudson,[20] or of Columbus or Cabot as having discovered America (a name probably not given to the continent till 1507).[21] That we are not without warrant for this supposition is shown by the following facts:

a. The bilingual Babylonian inscriptions are full of these twofold designations of the same place or country.

b. The triple-inscription of Behistun and the Aramaic translation of the same often give us four different names for the same country.[22]

c. The Elephantine of the Greeks was *ābu*[23] in Egyptian, and *Yeb* in our Aramaic text.

---

[19] The law was to be read to the people (Deut. 31:11) and according to Neh. 8:8 it was explained (מפרש) to them.

[19a] The name of the city is now Istanbul, but Dr. Wilson's argument holds. We may today speak of Istanbul as "—having been from the time of the glory of Greece the busy center of commercial activity—."

[20] Scribner's *History of the United States*, I, p. 30.

[21] *Idem* I, 127 f.

[22] Thus the Persian gives Armenia as *Armina*, the Susian as *Harminuya*, the Babylonian as *Uraštu* and the Aramaic as אררט. The name for Babylon is given as *Babirush* in the Persian, *Ba-pi-li* in the Susian, and in Babylonian is written in two different ways, while on other inscriptions it is written in at least four additional ways.

[23] See the inscription from the tomb of *Her-Khuf* at Assouan. *Ābu* in Egyptian means elephant, the Greek Elephantine being simply a translation.

d. In the Old Testament itself two names are sometimes used for the same city or country.[24]

e. The Jewish translators of the Old Testament did not hesitate to render the proper names of places by terms which conveyed the proper location to the people for whose benefit the translation was made. Thus the authors of the Greek Septuagint frequently render Philistines by *Allophuloi*; Misraim and Ham by *Aegyptos*. The Targum of Onkelos gives different terms to more than 20 names of places mentioned in the Pentateuch, besides giving translations of the names of more than 20 others.[25] The Samaritan Targum has about 120 proper names, mostly names of places and nations, that are given differently from what we find them in the Hebrew Masoretic text.[26] The Peshitto translation, also, used all of these liberties with the proper names.[27]

From these analogies we are justified in concluding that the mere presence in documents of the Old Testament of certain geographical terms of later origin than the rest of the documents is not conclusive proof that the mass of the documents is as late as the terms so used. It may be simply an evidence of editing for the sake of making the documents intelligible to the persons for whom they were designed.[28]

THE HISTORICAL DATA

As to the historic character of the Old Testament records in general there are no reasonable grounds for doubting it.

---

[24] Thus, מצרים and חם (for Egypt), Hebron and Kirjath-Arba, Salem and Jerusalem.

[25] See Brederik's *Konkordanz zum Targum Onkelos.*

[26] So, according to the concordance in my possession; some of these names are translations from Hebrew into Aramaic; some are the Greek equivalents of the Hebrew which have been taken over into the Aramaic.

[27] This is evident in a comparison of the proper names of Gen. 10 and 11. Here we find Cappadocia for Caphtor, Sepharvaim for Sippar, *Ain d' ebrroye* for *'yye ha'barim, Rametha* for *Pisgah.*

[28] A good example of such editing is to be found in certain changes made in the King James Version in the Tercentenary Edition of the Oxford Press, where, for example, the word "prevent" of the 1611 editions has been changed to "anticipate," "go before," etc.

For:

1. The language in which the different documents are written corresponds with the claim of the documents as to the time and place in which they were written. The first chapters of Genesis and Daniel are fullest of words derived from the Babylonian, as would be expected in records derived from Ur of the Chaldees and Babylon. The records concerning the patriarchs who are said to have lived in Egypt are the ones containing the most words of Egyptian origin. The Assyrian and Babylonian words occurring in the documents from the eighth century downward are mostly governmental terms and are such as would naturally be borrowed from the dominating races of the time. The Indo-European terms, whether Indian, Hittite, Medo-Persian, or Greek, appear in documents which were written in the times from Solomon onward, when the commercial and military relations of the Hebrews with the peoples speaking the languages from which the terms are borrowed would lead us to expect the influx of the new and foreign words to express the new ideas which they connote.

As to the Aramaic loan words, not one can be proved to be present in the Pentateuch, except in Genesis 31:47, where the Hebrew *Gal'eed* (Gilead) is stated to have been called by Laban *Yegar-sa'adutha,* of which compound the second word is certainly Aramaic. The existence of tribes speaking Aramaic can be proved from the monuments as far back as the Tel-el-Amarna letters.[29] The fact that there are more than a hundred explanations in Hebrew of Babylonian words in the Amarna Letters shows that Hebrew was understood at the court of the Egyptian kings, Amenophis III and IV. This confirms the Biblical account of the residence of Israelites in Egypt before the time of Moses.

2. As we have seen above,[30] the names, the order, and

---

[29] See Kraeling, *Aram and Israel.*
[30] Page 64 f.

the time of reigning of the different kings of the countries mentioned in the Old Testament harmonizes with what we find in the documents of Egypt, Babylon, Assyria, and other countries.[31] A harmony is found, also, in the statements made as to the relative power of these kings and the extent of their dominions.

3. We have already shown that the language, grammar, and literary forms are suitable to the respective ages in which the documents claim to have been written.

4. The civil, criminal, and constitutional laws also, both in their general character and in their literary forms, are in agreement with the times and circumstances when they are said to have been enunciated, or in use.[32] As to the ceremonial and ethical laws of the Old Testament, they are distinguished from those of all ancient peoples, especially by the fact that they are monotheistic and unicentral. That the ceremonial laws cannot have been derived from the other Semites is shown by the almost absolutely different vocabulary employed to express the acts and forms of religious service.[33] The vocabulary corroborates the statements of the records by showing that the Hebrew religion was of unique origin and of internal development.

5. That the Hebrew records which the critics assign to the post-Nehemiah period were written long before (as they purport to have been) is shown by the fact that the meanings of many of the terms in them were unknown when

---

[31] See for Damaskus, the article by Professor John D. Davis in the April number of the PTR for 1919 on "Hadadezer or Ben-Hadad."

[32] This statement is based on comparisons derived from the Code of Hammurabi and the laws of the Egyptians as gathered together in Révilloux's *Lois et Droits des Egyptiens.*

[33] See the author's articles on "Babylon and the Bible" in the *Pres. and Ref. Review* for 1902, and in *The Bible Student* for 1904. The dissimilarity in religious vocabulary which characterizes the Hebrew as compared with the Babylonian is apparent, also, as between the Hebrew on the one hand and the Phoenician and various Aramaic dialects on the other.

the earliest translations were made. Even at the time when the Septuagint was made, many meanings of Hebrew roots seem to have been unknown to them.[34] This is shown by the frequent transliterations found in that version. It seems inexplicable, also, that the different translators of the Pentateuch should have varied so much as they do in the rendition of many of the terms to denote animals, articles of clothing, drugs, implements, etc., if these parts had been written in postcaptivity times, when Aramaic was spoken by many of the Jews and understood by all the educated among them.

6. That some of the headings of the Psalms are not rendered in the LXX would indicate that the songs, instruments, times of circumstances to which they refer had passed out of the memory and tradition of the Jews. If the headings had been inserted after the Greek version was made, it is hard to see how the later Jews, who made the Targums and Talmuds, should not have understood their sense.[35]

7. Many undesigned coincidences support the historicity of the Old Testament. One of the most remarkable of these is the mention of the horse first in the history of Joseph, coincident with the appearance of the animal in the history of Western Asia and Egypt. Another is the failure to mention the elephant. If a large part of the Old Testament was written in the Greek period, it is noteworthy that this animal, which constituted the main arm of the military service from the time of Alexander down to the time of the Romans should never be noticed even in the Psalms which are alleged to be from Maccabean times. Especially is it noteworthy,

---

[34] See my article on "Lost Meanings of Hebrew Roots," in *Pres. and Ref. Review*, for 1892.

[35] That Psalms from the times of Moses and David may have been dated as we find them in the Bible is evident from the subscriptions of the Sumerian psalms from the time of Hammurabi. These subscriptions give at times the author, purpose, god addressed, tune, musical instruments and other notes similar to those found in the Psalter. See my articles in the PTR for 1926.

when we find the elephant playing so prominent a part in the wars of the Maccabees.

8. As to the appropriateness of the proper names of persons with the times in which they are said to have lived, the following may be said:

a. The names of persons in Genesis from Abraham to Joseph inclusive are in general such as the documents from the time of Hammurabi and from Egypt would lead us to expect. Some of them have not as yet been found outside of the Scriptures, but in every case these exceptions have their parallels in form or sense in the documents of the pre-Mosaic age.[36]

b. The names of persons from David to Ezra are entirely in harmony with the names to be expected and such as are found in the documents from Samaria, Moab, Assyria, and elsewhere.[36a]

c. For the times between Joseph and David too little is known from extra-Biblical documents to enable anyone to make a successful attack on the appropriateness of the names of persons mentioned in the Old Testament records.[36aa]

9. Attacks upon the genuineness and authority of the history because it contains accounts of miracles will be made by those only who are unacquainted with ancient historic records. Whether what they thought to be miracles were really miracles, and wherein the miracles consisted, are proper subjects of investigation, but no one can successfully dispute that all ancient peoples believed in them and that all ancient records are full of accounts of them.[37] In fact,

[36] See Langdon's *Sumerian and Babylonian Psalms.*

[36a] This fact has now been strikingly confirmed with respect to the orthography of personal names during the time of Jeremiah, by the discovery of the Lachish Letters. See Harry Torczyner: *The Lachish Letters,* Lachish 1, The Wellcome Archaeological Research Expedition to the Near East, 1938.

[36aa] The name Shamgar may be Hurrian; the name Araunah is Hurrian (II Sam. 24:16).

[37] See my article in the *Bible Student* for 1903.

so much is this the case that a historic record claiming to be ancient which contained no account of supposed miracles mighty justly be suspected of being a forgery of later times.[37a]

10. In like manner, he who rejects a document merely because it contains what purport to be apocalypses, or predictions, ignores the spirit, beliefs and practices of pre-Christian times.[38] Whether a document is, or contains, a prediction and what the prediction means and whether and how it was fulfilled, are all proper subjects of investigation. But all ancient history reveals clearly that the nations believed sincerely in the possibility and in the fact of the revelation of the will of the God or gods whom they worshiped. None but a deist, or an atheist, will deny their possibility. Theists must admit that they may have occurred. Christians will believe that the probability of their occurrence is involved in the mission of Jesus, the Word made flesh, through whom God in these latter days hath spoken unto us as in old times He spake through the prophets.[38a] Attacks upon Isaiah, Daniel, and other books, because they abound in wonderful predictions, will have weight only with those who deny the fundamentals of Christianity. To one who believes in the Lord and Saviour, Jesus Christ, the Son of God, and in the preparation of the world for His coming, the predictions of the Old Testament are but the glimmerings of rosy-fingered dawn before the full-orbed sun bursts forth as the light of a darkened world.

[37a] It must be stressed however that the miracles recorded in Scripture are unique, and differ essentially from other so-called miracles and miracle stories. The real objection is not that "wonder" stories are recorded in the Bible but that they are truly supernatural in character.

[38] See my article on "Jonah" and on "What does 'the sun stood still' mean?" in the PTR for 1918.

[38a] This statement should be stronger. Christians believe that these predictions occurred and that they were fulfilled for the simple reason that the infallible Scripture so declares.

11. The objections made to the genuineness of certain parts of the Old Testament upon the ground that they contain ideas found in extra-Biblical literature only in documents from an age later than the supposed date of the Biblical document might be taken with seriousness if they were made by an atheist or deist, but when made by one who claims to be a theist and to believe in a revelation, and when they occur in what purports to be a revelation, they seem too puerile to be even considered with patience and equanimity. What! Must Jehovah have derived His ideas of the resurrection from the Persians? Whence then did they derive them? And what care I for their ideas more than for those of Plato or other wise men of the past and present? I know nothing. They know nothing. Things that are equal to the same thing, etc. And yet, the critics deny the authorship of Isaiah 24—27 by Isaiah, and assert that Daniel is later than the fifth century B.C., on the ground among others, that the future resurrection is predicted in these documents on the authority of God. Oh, mortal man, canst thou bind the cords of Orion, or set a bound to the wisdom and foreknowledge of the Almighty?[39]

12. The most specious objection made to the Mosaic date and historical character of the Pentateuch is based upon the infrequent references to the laws, especially those of H and P, found in the Books of Judges, Samuel, and Kings; and further, upon the fact that the observances noted are often contrary to the requirements of the law. The force of this objection is broken by the following considerations, to wit: that the purpose of the Books of Judges, Samuel, and Kings, the critics themselves being witnesses, was not to give us a history of the religious institutions of Israel. "The stories of the deliverance of Israel represent only certain glorious moments in the history of these centuries."[40] "The

---

[39] See my article on *Apocalypses* and the *Date of Daniel* in PTR for 1921.
[40] Reader! Stop here and read Job 38-41.

subject of the Book of Samuel is the creation of a united Israel by Samuel, Saul, and David."[41] With this purpose in mind the authors generally make allusions to the law and the religious institutions and observances only insofar as they affect the history of the kings and nations whose fortunes it is the aim of the author to describe and moralize upon. The rule of conduct for the people they rightly find in the codes of E and D and in the words of the prophets. On the other hand, the Book of Chronicles was a history meant to confine itself "to matters still interesting to the theocracy of Zion, keeping Jerusalem and the temple in the foreground, and developing the divine pragmatism of the history, with reference, not so much to the prophetic word as to the fixed legislation of the Pentateuch (especially the Priests' Code), so that the whole narrative might be made to teach that Israel's glory lies in the observance of the divine law and ritual."[42] Keeping in mind the difference in purpose on the part of the writer of Chronicles it is easy to understand his frequent references to the laws of H and P as well as to those of E and D. Judges, Samuel, and Kings give an epitome of the history of Israel primarily from the political and moral side; Chronicles, primarily from the legal and religious side.[43] The conquest, the wars, the erection of the temple as the symbol of the unity of Israel, the division of the kingdom and the history of the two parts of it, and the final destruction of both kingdoms with the causes and manner thereof, constituted the subject matter of the prophetic history; the priestly writer on the other hand, gives the history of the kings and of the nations only as a background to his picture of the ecclesiastical and liturgical development of Israel based upon the prescriptions of the law of Moses. The prophetical writers dwell more upon the

---

[41] G. F. Moore in *Enc. Bib.*, p. 2641.
[42] W. Robertson Smith and Ed. König in *Enc. Bib.*, p. 2664.
[43] W. R. Smith and S. R. Driver in *Enc. Bib.*, p. 765.

breaches of the laws, the priestly writer more upon the observance of them. In order to maintain their assertion that the laws of H and P are not mentioned in the history, the critics must and do deny the reliability of the history recorded in Chronicles. The force of their objection, therefore, depends upon the ability of the critics to establish the unhistorical character of the material facts recorded in the works of Ezra, Nehemiah, and Chronicles insofar as they give information additional to, or in apparent conflict with what we find in the older books. The precarious character of the evidences for the date of a document to be used from the use of the names and designations of God is to be seen in the collections of such names gathered from the Koran, the New Testament, and the Apocryphal and Pseudepigraphical literature of the Jews.[44]

13. The evidence derived from recent extra-Biblical studies shows that there is no sufficient ground for holding that the Book of Daniel was not written at or near Babylon in the latter part of the sixth century B.C., as the prima-facie evidence of the book itself indicates.[45]

14. A thorough study of the language of the Book of Jonah shows that it was most probably written in the eighth century B.C. Since the mission of the prophet was to the people of Nineveh, there is no reason why he should have given the name of the king of Assyria. The *king* of Nineveh may have been simply the mayor of the city. There are two good reasons why we should not expect to find the repentance of the Ninevites recorded on the monuments of Assyria. First, there are very meager documents of any kind from the time when Jonah is said to have lived. Second, the Assyrian mon-

---

[44] See PTR for 1919-21.
[45] See my article on *The Aramaic of Daniel* in *Biblical and Theological Studies by the Members of the Faculty of Princeton Theological Seminary* (Scribner's 1912), my *Studies in the Book of Daniel* (Putnam's 1916); and the PTR for 1917-1924.

archs scarcely ever record anything prejudicial to their own dignity or glory. Third, the Psalm in chapter 2 is not made up of excerpts from late Psalms; but on the contrary is one of the most original and unique pieces of literature in existence, both as to subject and vocabulary.[46]

15. As to the conclusion of the radical critics that the Books of Chronicles, Ezra, and Nehemiah are unreliable, the following may be said:

a. It is based upon the assumption that the writers had as sources nothing but the present books of the Old Testament from Genesis to Kings inclusive, supplemented by certain postexilic works which have long since perished. Since it is admitted by all that the earlier documents of the Old Testament, such as J, E, D, Samuel, Hosea, Amos, and the sources of Kings, passed unscathed through the fire and destruction accompanying the fall of Samaria and Jerusalem, it cannot be assumed that other records also may not have been preserved. The Chronicler himself asserts that he had access to such sources, or at least to works derived from such sources. No other writer of the Old Testament cites his authorities so frequently and so explicitly. That he recasts his material in his own style and language and with remarks and comments of his own, no more invalidates the reliability of his facts than do similar methods in the case of Gibbon, Prescott, and Mommsen. That he inserts his own notes and comments no more throws doubt on his citation of facts that is true in the case of the Books of Kings.

Against the express statements of authorities given by the Chronicler, what evidence have the critics to produce? Nothing but conjectures. Nothing but surmises and opinions based on their own ignorance and the silence of other records. Are the critics going to maintain that many works of precaptivity times did not survive the destruction of Jerusa-

---

[46] See articles on Jonah in PTR for 1917.

lem and afterward perish? How then about the sources of
Kings? Are they going to maintain that all the works ever
written have been cited in the books older than Chronicles,
that the *Book of Jasher* and the *Book of the Wars of Jehovah* are the only ones that have disappeared? How about
the 3,000 proverbs of Solomon and his 1,005 songs?[47] How
about the records of the kings of Israel and Judah as to which
it is said so often in Kings that the rest of the deeds of the
kings were written in them? "If," as Dr. Driver says,[48] "it
was not the Chronicler's intention to pervert the history,"
why should he have invented or perverted the sources from
which he claims to get his information? The present-day
critics, living just about 2,300 years after the Chronicler
wrote his books, may dispute about his statements and deny
his facts, and even the existence of the documents which he
cites; but most sensible men without preconceived opinions
will probably agree with me that the Chronicler is more
likely to have been right and to have told the truth, especially
about the records which he used, than any man today. The
testimony of the Chronicler cannot be overthrown by the
opinion of anyone now living.

b. It is not fair to reject one or both of the two apparently
irreconcilable statements because *we* cannot explain them.
Sometimes apparent difficulties can be removed by a change
of the pointing or interpretation of the original Hebrew.[49]
Sometimes the objections are based on an interpretation of

---

[47] There are only 915 verses in our whole Book of Proverbs. The men of
Hezekiah extracted chapters 25-29 (138 verses) from these 3,000 proverbs of
Solomon. What became of the others?

[48] LOT, 533.

[49] Thus וישב in I Kings 12:2 may be pointed and read as "and he returned"
or as "and he dwelt." מת in II Kings 23:30 may be rendered "dying" rather
than "dead" and so be made to harmonize with II Chron. 35:24, where it is
said that Josiah died in Jerusalem.

the original which creates a discrepancy where none really exists.[50]

c. One of the most serious charges made against the Chronicler is that he exaggerates in his numerical statements. Thus, he makes the army of Jeroboam I to be 800,000 and that of Abijah 400,000; Zera with 1,000,000 men meets Asa with 580,000; and Jehoshaphat has an army of 1,160,000. If, however, this is an argument against the historicity of Chronicles, it may be used also against Samuel and Kings; for the Philistines have 30,000 chariots (I Sam. 13:5), David slew 40,000 horsemen of the Syrians in one battle (II Sam. 10:18), Joab numbered 800,000 men of Israel and 500,000 of Judah (II Sam. 24:9), Solomon had 40,000 stalls of horses (I Kings 5:6 [4:24]), Rehoboam had 180,000 chosen men which were warriors (I Kings 12:21), and the children of Israel slew 100,000 Syrians in one day (I Kings 20:29). And it cannot be maintained that the Chronicler exaggerated regularly the numbers as given in Kings, since in the 17 cases, where

---

[50] Thus, it is said that there is an inexplicable disagreement between the account of Athaliah's overthrow as given in II Kings 11:4 f. and that given in II Chron. 23:1 f. This assumed disagreement is based primarily upon the assumption that the *Kāri* (כרי) and runners of Kings could not have been Levites as Chronicles would seem to demand. Doubt, however, as to the meaning of *Kāri* is manifest, when we see that Gesenius, in his *Thesaurus* (671 b), gives four meanings as being upheld by various scholars, to which may be added several from the versions and one or two from recent scholars. If we connect it with the Assyrian *karu* "to cut," a synonym of *karatu*, it will be a synonym of כרתי, and mean "executioner" like *ṭabbaḥ* in Gen. 34:1. If we connect it with the Assyrian *kararu*, a synonym of *eteru* and *šuzubu* "to surround, either for protection or capture" (Muss-Arnolt 25 b), it might well mean "body-guard." The פלתי, so frequently used with כרתי, may be connected with the Assyrian *pultu, paštu* "sword." Compare Syriac *pusta* "ascia, securis." That runners might be Levites, and even priests, is shown by the fact that Ahimaaz, David's runner, was a son of Zadok the priest (II Sam. 18:19 f.). Until the meaning of these terms has been fixed, we are justified merely in saying that some of the details of the account are not clear to us. This does not mean that they are not true.

the numbers differ as between the two books, the text of Kings is greater in five and that of the Chronicler in 12.[51]

In view, then, of the fact that the prophetical history, as well as the priestly, contains these large enumerations, it seems best to maintain either that the enumerations are correct, or that they have been corrupted in the course of transmission. We are not so sure as some seem to be that they are not correct. We are not to look upon the armies of those days as composed of drilled troops like the Macedonian phalanxes, or the Roman legions, but as levies en masse, embracing all the people from about 14 to 20 years of age and upward, a whole nation in arms. Every man was interested in the wars, because defeat meant death or captivity to all alike. Besides, they were fighting at their own doorsteps and for their hearths and homes. When we think of the enormous disciplined armies which single cities such as Nineveh, Damascus, Tyre, Ekron, Gaza, Sparta, and Rome used to put into the field, we may well pause before affirming with such assurance as some do that the figures of the Books of Kings and Chronicles are incredible. But, if some think they are incredible, let them remember that numbers, especially when denoted by a system of notation, are the hardest of all facts to transmit correctly. There is usually nothing in the context to preserve them from corruption. They may have been misread in the original sources or changed in the course of copying; but only those who have never engaged in the study of manuscripts will indict a whole document simply because some of the numerical notations are beyond the possibility of being read with certainty or accepted as original.

---

[51] In Sennacherib's Prism Inscription I, 34-50, there are eight numerical statements. In six of these the numbers vary in the different versions. In the Babylonian and Aramaic versions of the Behistun inscription of Darius the numbers differ in almost every case. Yet these versions are contemporaneous. See PTR for 1914.

d. In order to prove the untrustworthiness of the Chronicler, an attempt is made to show that his work was not written till about 300 B.C. The first proof of this is said to be found in I Chronicles 3. The text of this passage is admitted to vary so much that commentators are not sure whether six or 13 generations are meant. According to Dr. Driver, the Hebrew text gives six generations from Zerubbabel onward. If we place him at 520 B.C. and count 20 years to a generation, this will bring us to 400 B.C., as the date of the book. Twenty years to a generation is a good Oriental average.[52]

e. It is an absurd argument against the historicity of the Books of Chronicles, that they give information not found in the Books of Samuel and Kings. Why should the author have written the Chronicles at all, if he had had the same design and gave the same information as the authors of Samuel and Kings? It is perfectly proper and natural, also, that he should have written especially about Levites, singers, and festivals; since, as the critics rightly affirm, he was looking at things from a priestly standpoint.

No one can deny that the temple was built by Solomon, and that the plans and, in large measure, the materials for the structure were prepared by David. This temple was intended for the worship of the God of Israel. This worship consisted in sacrifices, prayers and praises. The service required large numbers of priests, servants, and singers; and they must have been organized, so that everything should be conducted in decency and order. The Chronicles say that David organized these services of the temple. Why deny that he did this most sensible and fitting thing?

Now, when this temple was first built, all that would be necessary would be to take over the priests and the ritual

---

[52] See Assayuti's *History of the Califs,* where generations are often only for 16 or 18 years.

already in existence and vary them only insofar as was required to meet the new conditions of an enlarged and more dignified place of worship. The old priesthood of the temple at Shiloh and the old laws of the tabernacle with reference to sacrifices and festivals would be found sufficient; but to make the service more efficient and suitable to the great glory of the magnificent house that had been erected for the God of Israel, certain new regulations as to the time and manner of the services were instituted by David. Whatever is not referred to as having originated with him must be presumed to have been already in existence.

Since David and Solomon built the temple, it is common sense to suppose that they organized the priests into regular orders for the orderly service of the sanctuary. These priests had already had their clothing prescribed by Moses after the analogy of the Egyptian and all other orders of priesthood the world over. He also had prescribed the kinds and times of offerings and the purpose for which they were offered. The Israelites, also, like the Egyptians and Babylonians, had for their festive occasions such regulations as are attributed to David for the observance of these festivals, so as to avoid confusion and to preserve decency in the house of God.

AN INCONSISTENT THEORY MADE TO FIT

Is it to be supposed that on these festive occasions no music was to be employed and no hymns of praise to God to be sung? Even the most savage tribes have music at their festivals and we know that the ancient Egyptians had numerous hymns to Amon and other gods, and that the Assyrians and Babylonians, and even the Sumerians before them, delighted in singing psalms of praise and penitence as a part of their ritual of worship.[53] These hymns in all cases were

---

[53] See the long list of hymns to Amon and Aton given in Breasted's *Egypt*, V, 133. The authors of some of these hymns are given. *Idem* Thotmes III and

accompanied by instrumental music. Some of the Sumerian, Babylonian and Egyptian hymns were current in writing for hundreds, or even thousands, of years before the time of Solomon; and some musical instruments had existed for the same length of time. Are we to suppose that the Hebrews alone among the nations of antiquity had no vocal and instrumental music in their temple services? The critics maintain that poetry is the earliest form of expression of a people's thoughts and history. Many of them assert that the song of Deborah antedates all other literary productions in the Bible. Most of them will admit that David composed the lament over Saul and Jonathan.

But they draw the line at his Psalms of praise and penitence.[54] Why? Because it suits their theory that the Psalms were prepared for use in the second temple. They hold at the same time that certain poems, like the songs of Deborah and Miriam and the blessings of Jacob and Moses, antedate by centuries the historical narratives in which they are found, but that the Psalms were all, or nearly all, composed after captivity. What grounds have they for holding such seemingly inconsistent theories? Absolutely none that is based on any evidence, unless the wish to have it so, in order to bolster up their conception of the history of Israel's religion, be called evidence.[54a]

Merenptah, kings of Egypt, both wrote hymns. *Idem* Assurbanipal, king of Assyria, also wrote hymns. See Streck's *Assurbanipal* III, 342 f. That the ancient Sumerians at, or before, the time of Abraham sometimes gave the name of the author of a psalm may be seen in Langdon's *Sumerian and Babylonian Psalms*, pp. 287, 317.

[54] See pages 229-239 of Frank's *Studien zur Babylonischen Religion;* Langdon's *Sumerian and Babylonian Psalms;* Erman's *Aegypten und Aegyptisches Leben im Altertum,* II, 350-412; Wilkinson, *The Ancient Egyptians,* I, 431-500.

[54a] It is interesting to observe that at the present the postexilic date for the Psalter is more and more being abandoned and numerous Psalms are being assigned to pre-exilic times. The impetus to this shift in emphasis is to be found in Babylonian poems and in Ugaritic, and this new position is being prosecuted very largely by Scandinavian scholars. See Appendix 2e.

PSALM WRITERS WOULD NOT HAVE ABSURDLY ATTRIBUTED

THEIR WORK TO PRECAPTIVITY AUTHORS

Of course, it is obvious that music is mentioned in the Books of Kings; but it is made prominent in Chronicles, and the headings of many of the Psalms attribute them to David and in three cases to Moses or Solomon. It is hardly to be supposed that the writer of these headings would make his work absurd by making statements that his contemporaries would have known to be untrue. Whether the headings are all trustworthy, or not, it is absurd to suppose that the writers of them would have attributed so many of the Psalms to precaptivity authors, when their contemporaries must have known that the whole body of Psalms had arisen after the fall of the first temple, had such been actually the case. The most natural supposition would be that David either made or collected a sufficient number of Psalms to meet the requirements of worship in the temple which Solomon was about to build.

As to the text of the headings of the Psalms, the evidence of the manuscripts and versions goes to show that they are not merely substantially the same as they were in the third century B.C., but that most of them must even then have been hoary with age. Even when the Septuagint version was made, the meanings of many of the terms used in the headings were already unknown, and the significance of many words and phrases had passed out of mind. A large proportion of the names is not to be found in later Hebrew and in no Aramaic dialect. Besides the roots of many of these words have closer analogies in Babylonian than in any other language.

All this would suggest that their origin must go back to the times of Ezra and Nehemiah or to the captivity; and that they, in whole or in part, came down from the usages and administration of Solomon's temple. There is no reason for supposing that the Psalms and their headings may not have been present intact through all the confusion and destruction of the fall of Jerusalem, inasmuch as the sources of Samuel and Kings (and the works of most of the prophets) were admittedly so present. Besides, the Hebrew manuscripts and all of the great ancient primary versions agree almost absolutely with the text of our ordinary Hebrew Bibles and their English versions in attributing 73 of the Psalms to David as the author or subject of the respective Psalms. The Greek edition of Swete agrees in attributing to David every one of the 73. The edition of the Latin Gallican version of Harden[55] (*Psalterium juxta Hebraeos Hieronymi*, edited with introduction and *Apparatus Criticus* by J. M. Harden, D.D., LL.D., Trinity College, Dublin; London, Macmillan Co., 1922) agrees in all but Psalm 22; where, however, E and H, two of the best manuscripts, do agree. The Syriac-Peshitto version of Walton's *Polyglot* agrees in regard to all, except Psalms 13, 39, and 124.[56] And the Aramaic of Walton's *Polyglot* ascribes to David every one of the 73, except 122, 131, and 133.

It will be noted that all the five texts, the Hebrew and its four great ancient versions, agree that 66 out of the 73 psalms were either written by, or for, or concerning David[57]

---

[55] Temples imply both singers and songs. In II Sam. 22:1, David is said to have spoken the words of Psalm 18. In II Sam. 23:1, he is called the sweet psalmist of Israel. Critics generally admit that he wrote the lament over Saul and Jonathan. Why then may he not have written the psalms attributed to him in the headings of the psalms? And why may not he, like Watts and Cooper and Wesley and Havergal, have himself produced, or at least collected, a whole psalm book? The temple requires singers; singers require songs; David supplies songs. Chronicles and the headings of the psalms state that the Israelites had in the psalms of David and the singers of the temple just what common sense demands that they must have had.

[56] In the case of Psalms 55 and 62 David occurs in the headings, though he is not specifically stated to have been the author.

[57] The detailed evidence as to the headings of the Psalms has appeared in the PTR for January and July, 1926, where the secondary versions of the Sep-

(the Hebrew preposition *l* may mean "by," "for," or "concerning"), and that four out of five of these agree in regard to all the 73.

Finally, a striking and almost convincing testimony for the early date of most of the psalms lies in the fact that, except in a very few cases, we find no definite allusions in them to events or persons later than the time of Solomon.

Thus, common sense and universal analogy compel us to believe that an orderly worship conducted by priests in accordance with prescribed regulations and a service of song commensurate with the dignity and decency becoming the house of God must have existed among the Hebrews, certainly from the time that the first temple was constructed and probably from the time that the tabernacle was erected and the annual festivals established. Historians of royal courts, of diplomacy and war, like the author of the Books of Kings, may not mention such things; but we may be sure that they existed. The temple itself proves this. Universal experience proves it. The weeping stone at the foundation of the temple, where the Jews of today congregate to bewail the long departed glories of Mount Zion and the glorious house of Israel's God, testifies that the traditions about the sweet psalmist of Israel were not all figments of the imagination, nor mythical creations of later times.

f. Another proof of the lateness of the Chronicler is said to be the mention of Jaddua as high priest in Nehemiah 12:11,22. It is assumed that this Jaddua is the same as the one mentioned by Josephus[58] as the high priest who went out to meet Alexander when he went up to Jerusalem. In-

---

tuagint—the Memphitic and the Sahidic Coptic, the Harklensian Syriac and the Syro-Palestinian, the Ethiopic, the Arabic, the Armenian, and the Latin Vulgate have also been considered.

[58] *Antiquities*, XI, 8:4.

asmuch as this expedition of Alexander is recorded by Josephus alone and said by the critics never to have occurred, and as the particular Jaddua who is said by Josephus to have met Alexander is mentioned nowhere else either by Josephus or by any other ancient writer, we fail to see the force of this argument. For, if Josephus invented the story about Alexander, he may have invented his Jaddua, too. But granting that there was a Jaddua at 336 B.C., or thereabout, we fail to see why he may not have been high priest for 70 or even 80 years. Having had a great-grandfather who lived to be hale and hearty at 105, and a great-grandmother to be 99, and three great-uncles to be 94, 96, and 101 respectively, with about a dozen other relatives, no farther away than a great-uncle, who lived to be from 75 to 92, and all *compos mentis,* and most active in body till almost the end, the writer of this article can see nothing improbable in the Jaddua of Josephus having been the same as the Jaddua of Ezra.

g. The newest weapon of proof, however, that has been forged against the historicity of the Chronicler is that which has been produced in the arsenal of Oxford by Drs. Driver and Gray. The great German critic Ewald asserted that it was both unnecessary and contrary to contemporary usage for the kings of Persia to be given the title king of Persia, while as yet there were kings of Persia; and that consequently the Hebrew documents employing this title must have been written after kings of Persia had ceased to exist. If this were absolutely true, it would bring down to Greek times the composition of Chronicles, Ezra, Nehemiah, and Daniel, since they all contain the title. It is a sufficient answer to this assertion to say that 18 different authors in 19 different documents from Persian times use this title altogether 38 different times, and of at least six different Persian kings; that it is used of Cyrus seven years before the conquest of

Babylon in 539 B.C. and of Artaxerxes III about 365 B.C.; that it is used in Persian, Susian, Babylonian, Greek, Aramaic, and Hebrew; that it was used in Media, Babylonia, Asia Minor, Greece, and Palestine, and according to Herodotus in Ethiopia; and that it is used in letters, dates and other like documents of the Scriptures just as it is used in the extra-Biblical documents. Further, it has been shown that it was not common for authors of the Greek period to use the title.[59]

---

[59] See my articles in the PTR for 1904-5 and for 1917, and in the *Sachau Denkschrift*, Berlin, 1912.

In addition to what Dr. Wilson has written we may note that Ariyaramna, at least fifty years before the Persians took Babylon, says, "Ariyaramna the great king, the king of kings, the Persian king."

VI

THE EVIDENCE: Religion

BEFORE CLOSING this succinct review of the lines of defense of the Old Testament Scriptures, we must emphasize briefly the strongest bulwark of them all, the undeniable uniqueness and superlative clearness and importance of the religious ideas contained in them.

A study of the religious systems of the Egyptians, Babylonians, and other ancient peoples, has revealed to us a groping after God, if haply they might find Him; but nowhere among all the nations is it recorded that a clear apprehension of one living and true God — the creator and preserver, the guide, the judge, the Saviour, and the sanctifier of His people — was attained. Other religions are outward, concerned with words and deeds. Their sins are offenses or delinquencies, their substitutions are material equivalents, their atonements are physical purifications, their resurrection is a groundless expectation, their judgment is without mercy, their immortality consigns to darkness and dust, and a future life of joy is at best for the few and great. The Old Testament religion is essentially inward. It is the religion of the mind and heart, of love, joy, *faith,* hope, and salvation through the grace of God alone. How account for this religion? It must have come either by derivation, evolution, or revelation. The prophets say it came from God. No other theory of its origin can account for its uniqueness and its results, its superiority and its influence. The prophets and their ideas are facts in evidence, which all the quibbling of the critics cannot impugn. The prophets say they had their ideas from God. If not, whence? It cannot have come by derivation; for none of the other nations had the same ideas of God, creation, sin, and redemption.[1] If it came by revelation, the greatest of all miracles has happened involving all the rest. For if God spake through the prophets, His revelations of His will could not have been bound by the shackles of time and circumstance. The prophets who spake for Him spake not merely as the men of their own time, but as men of all time, as men who were spokesmen of Him who knows the end from the beginning, and has all power in Heaven and on earth. The canon of the modern critical school that treats the prophets as the creatures of their time is antagonistic to this fundamental conception of the prophets' mission as it was enunciated by the prophets themselves. They say God spake *to* them and they spake *for* God.[1a] The critics say that they gave utterance to the spirit of the times (the *Zeitgeist*) and that they were limited by the time and place of their birth. But, if this were all the source of their information, how then did it come, that not from the oracles of Thebes and Memphis, nor from the temples of Babylon, nor from

---

[1] That it could not have been derived from the Babylonians, see my articles in the *Presbyterian and Reformed Review* for 1902 and the *Bible Student* for 1904.

[1a] Those who would adequately explain the prophetic movement must account for at least three factors, 1.) the psychological fact of the prophets' conviction that God had actually spoken to them; 2.) the continuity of the movement, consisting of men who lived over a period of several hundred years, all believing that God had spoken to them and 3.) the teleological trend of the predictions (Messianic prophecy). In all the nations of antiquity there is no real parallel to the prophetic movement.

the sacred precincts of Delphi, nor from the Sibyls and augurs of Rome, but from the deserts of Midian, and from the sheepfolds of Tekoa, and from the dungeons of Zedekiah, and from the lowly cots of captives on the banks of the Chebar and the Euphrates, came forth those magic words of hope and salvation and glory for a sin-cursed world that have made the desert hearts of all who heard them to rejoice and blossom like the rose in the sunlight of God's favor, in the revivifying atmosphere of His presence? God with us! This is the key to unlock the mysterious chambers of the Old Testament.

VII

Conclusion

B UT THE TIME HAS COME to conclude this summary of
evidence for the defense in the case of the critics against
the Old Testament. We hope that the evidence adduced
will be sufficient to show that the general reliability of the
Old Testament documents has not been impaired by recent
discoveries outside the Old Testament. The literary forms
are in harmony with what comparative literature would
lead us to expect. The civil, criminal, and constitutional
laws agree with what the civilization of the ancient nations
surrounding Palestine would presuppose; while the ceremonial, moral, and religious laws are differentiated from
those of others by their genesis in a monotheistic belief
and a divine revelation. The use of writing in the age of
Moses and Abraham is admitted by all and the existence
of the Hebrew language in the time of the Exodus is assured by the glosses of the Amarna Letters, as well as by
the proper names on the Egyptian and Babylonian monuments. The general correctness of the Hebrew text that
has been transmitted to us is established beyond just grounds
of controversy. The morphology, syntax, and meaning of
the language of the various books conform with what the
face of the documents demands. The chronological and

162

geographical statements are more accurate and reliable than those afforded by any other ancient documents; and the biographical and other historical narratives harmonize marvelously with the evidence afforded by extra-Biblical documents.

We therefore send this volume forth with the prayer that it may strengthen the faith of those who still believe in God and in Jesus Christ His Son. We need not and do not fear the truth about the Bible. We welcome all sincere and honest study of its origin, purpose, and meaning. But is it too much to ask and hope that more of those who have been appointed by the Church to teach its history and its doctrines should devote their time and energies to the defense of its great and fundamental, unique and outstanding, facts and implications, rather than to the picking of flaws in the garments of the prophets and to the punching of holes in the robe of Christ's perfection? It may not be ours to remove all the difficulties, to harmonize all the apparent inconsistencies, to explain all the mysteries, and to solve all the problems of the Old Testament; but we can show at least, that we believe that Christ and the apostles are more likely to be right than we, that the age-long judgment of the Church with respect to the Bible may after all be right, and that our business is to defend with all lawful means the citadel of faith rather than to join the hosts of the infidel in the assaults upon its walls.

APPENDIXES

1. *The Masoretic Vocalization*

A FURTHER WORD should be said about the importance of the Masoretic vocalization. In order to understand this vocalization a few preliminary remarks must be made with respect to the kind of syllables that appear in Hebrew. In the following word there are three syllables.

$$\overset{2}{\text{d}^{\text{e}}} - \overset{}{b\text{a}} - \overset{1}{\text{riym}}$$

A syllable which ends in a consonant is said to be closed, whereas one which ends in a vowel is called open. The syllable -riym ends in a consonant and so is closed. It is also accented, and this fact is indicated by the bolder type. The syllable -ba, on the other hand, ends in a vowel and so is open. Inasmuch as it is written immediately before the accented syllable we shall call it a near (i. e., near to the accent) open syllable. The syllable dᵉ also ends in a vowel and is open. It, however, does not occur immediately, but two places before the accent. We shall, therefore, call it a distant open syllable. Any open syllable which is two or more syllables removed from the accent is a distant open syllable.

If we examine the Hebrew word qᵉ-ṭal-**tem**, we notice that it contains three syllables. The syllable in bold type is accented, the immediately preceding syllable is closed and unaccented, and the remaining syllable is distant open. In the above two words we have the following types of syllables: accented; unaccented closed; near open; distant open.

In the Semitic languages there are three basic vowels, *a*, *i*, and *u*, which appear both as long (unchangeable) *â*, *î*, *û*, and short, *a*, *i*, *u*. In Hebrew these vowels appear in different forms, depending upon the type of syllable in which they occur and its proximity to the accent of the word. The following chart will show how the long vowels appear in Hebrew:

CHART OF LONG VOWELS (UNCHANGEABLE)

a appears in Hebrew as *ô* or *â*.

i appears in Hebrew as *îy* or *î* (sometimes *ê*).

u appears in Hebrew as *û*.

These long vowels are not affected by changes in the position of the accent; they remain the same no matter what the type of syllable may be in which they are found. They may therefore be called *unchangeable* vowels.

The changes which the short vowels undergo may be illustrated by the following chart:

CHART OF SHORT VOWELS

Type of Syllable	*a*	*i*	*u*
Accented or Near Open	*ā*	*ē*	*ō*
Unaccented Closed	*a*	*i* or *e*	*u* or *o*
Distant Open	*C*e*	*C*e*	*C*e*

*Note: *C* stands for Consonant. The * represents Shewa.

By way of explanation we may note again the word de-*ba*-**riym**. This word contains the following vowels, da-*ba*-**riym** The accented syllable contains the vowel *i*, and since this vowel is unchangeable it appears, in accordance with the long vowel chart, as *iy*. The preceding syllable (*penult*) is near open and contains an *a* vowel. According to the short vowel chart this *a* vowel must appear in a near open syllable as *ā*, The preceding syllable is distant open with an *a* vowel, and the short vowel chart tells us that an *a* vowel in a distant open syllable must appear as *e*. Hence, the original vowels in da-*ba*-rim must be written in Hebrew as d*e*-*ba*-rîym, and this is exactly how the Masoretes have written the word.

Of what importance, however, is all this? It is of the utmost importance for it shows how faithfully the Masoretes have preserved the text and its pronunciation. When the words of the Hebrew text can be compared with corresponding words in the cognate languages, it will be shown that the orthography of the Hebrew words has been correctly preserved. For example, the Babylonians spelled the name of the city Megiddo as Ma-gid-dâ. How should this word be written in Hebrew? The two charts above will give us the answer. Let us begin with the last syllable (the ultima). *Da* contains a long *â*, and so should be written in Hebrew as *dô*. (It also receives the accent in Hebrew **dô**.) The preceding syllable *gid*, inasmuch as it is closed and unaccented, should appear in Hebrew either as *gid* or *ged*. The consonant *d*, however, is doubled, and therefore *gid* is to be preferred over *ged*.[1] The first syllable is distant open, *ma*, and the vowel *a* which it contains should, according to the short vowel chart, appear as *me*. This is precisely what we find in Hebrew, namely, the orthography, m*e*-gid-**dô**. This fact will enable the reader to appreciate somewhat the remarkable accuracy with which the text of the Hebrew Old Testament has been handed down to us. Here is unusually strong evidence that the Old Testament has been kept pure ". . . by His singular care and providence" (*The Westminster Confession of Faith*, Chapter I, viii).

The following is a brief list of words which appear in

---

[1] Before a doubled consonant (Daghesh Forte) *i* often appears in preference to *e*.

Arabic and Babylonian. The reader may examine each word, and with the aid of the charts figure out for himself how the word should be spelled in Hebrew. He may then check the results with the actual Hebrew orthography given below. It will be well to remember that each one-syllable word is accented, and each Hebrew word of more than one syllable given below is accented on the last syllable (ultima).[2]

Arabic	na-sa-mah	(breath)	becomes in Hebrew			nᵉ-šā-m**ā**h
"	na-bîy	(prophet)	"	"	"	nā-*b*îy
"	ab	(father)	"	"	"	ā*b*
"	udn	(ear)	"	"	"	ōzn
"	ma-qâm	(place)	"	"	"	mā-qôm
"	ba-ra-qah	(blessing)	"	"	"	bᵉ-rā-qāh
"	gub	(well)	"	"	"	gō*b*
Babylonian	giz	(shearing)	"	"	"	gēz
"	dam	(blood)	"	"	"	dām
"	tît	(clay)	"	"	"	ṭîṭ
"	ur	(light)	"	"	"	ōr

If the reader will study the above examples carefully he will be impressed with the faithful manner in which the Masoretic text of the Old Testament reflects the correct orthography of the words. It is of the utmost interest to notice how this information concerning the principles of the Masoretes supports the position which Dr. Wilson maintained, namely, the essential accuracy of the Masoretic text.[3]

2. *Modern Discovery and the Old Testament*

    a. *The Texts from Nuzi (Yorgan Tepe)*

Since Dr. Wilson's death, archaeology has greatly supported the position which he maintained with respect to the trustworthiness of the Old Testament. In this section of the Appendix we shall endeavor briefly to direct the reader's atten-

---

[2] The orthography of the words has been simplified for the benefit of the reader who is not acquainted with the Semitic languages.

[3] For the understanding of the basic philosophy of the Hebrew syllables and vowels the writer is indebted to Cyrus H. Gordon.

tion to some of the more important instances of this fact. We may begin with an account of the discovery in 1925 of the cuneiform documents of Nuzi, modern Yorgan Tepe (*blanket mound* — the language is Turkish). Nuzi was a center of the Hurrians who are probably to be identified with the Biblical Horites (see, e. g., Gen. 14:6). That the Horites were a historical people was a disputed point. Now, however, there would seem to be no question but that a center of Horite or Hurrian civilization had been discovered.

What is of particular interest is the unusual collection of cuneiform tablets which was found at Nuzi. For the most part these tablets are contract or business documents. The proper names which are found upon them are in large measure Hurrian proper names, and consequently they are of importance for an understanding of the Hurrian language. They have to do with a number of subjects, with the result that much is now known about the life of the ancient Hurrians. The tablets have proved to be of tremendous importance, and they have actually given the deathblow to the theory that the Book of Genesis does not present a trustworthy picture of the background of the narratives of the patriarchs.

It seems that in ancient Nuzi one could not buy land. If therefore one wished to obtain land, he had to engage in a device which was called "adoption." Many of the tablets of Nuzi are therefore known as adoption tablets. A man who wished to obtain a certain piece of land would have himself adopted by those who owned the land. They would legally adopt him as their son and heir and would deed the land to him. This was called *zittu* (inheritance share). In return for this act, the one adopted would give a gift (*qištu*) to those who had adopted him. Thus it was possible to acquire great possessions, and indeed, one man by the Hurrian name of Tehiptilla had himself adopted by many different persons.

In the light of these tablets from Nuzi many matters mentioned in the Book of Genesis receive their explanation. The passage, Genesis 15:2,3, has long been a *cruz interpretum*. It was the custom, we learn from the Nuzi documents, for a couple who were without children to adopt someone who in return for being made the heir would take care of them in their old age and see that they were given a decent burial. It seems that this was the function of Eleazar of Damascus. On the other hand if an heir should be born later, the adopted son would have to give way to this heir. Hence, we may understand the language of the Lord. "This man [i. e., Eleazar] shall not be thine heir; but he that shall come forth out of thine own bowels shall be thine heir" (Gen. 15:4, A.S.V.). Abraham was acting in accord with the customs of the time.

The episode of Hagar also receives illumination. When the legal wife was barren it was the custom for this wife to provide the husband with a concubine that seed might be raised up. One of the tablets may be rendered as follows:

> If Gilimninu does not bear children Gilimninu is to obtain a woman of n/Lullu-land as a wife for Shennima.

In this text Shennima is the husband and Gilimninu the wife. If the wife is barren it is her duty to provide for the husband a concubine from the land of Lullu, where the best slaves were obtained. One may note immediately the parallels with the account in Genesis. Sarah followed the custom of the day in taking a concubine for Abraham.[4] She, however, refused to continue to act in accordance with custom and became angry with Hagar. Sarah's action was in complete accord with the social practices of her day, and

---

[4] The practice also finds illustration in the Code of Hammurabi.

the same is true of Rachel's action later, when she gave Bilhah to Jacob (Gen. 30:3). It should be noted in passing that whereas these actions were perfectly in accord with custom, they were not for that reason morally defensible.

Sarah wished to drive out Hagar, and in this she was not acting in accord with custom. The Nuzi tablet, to which we have been making reference, goes on to say that Gilimninu is not to send the offspring away. Sarah therefore was violating custom, but we may notice that the Lord did speak to Abraham: "Let it not be grievous in thy sight, because of the lad, and because of thy handmaid; in all that Sarah saith unto thee, hearken unto her voice; for in Isaac shall thy seed be called" (Gen. 21:12, A.S.V.).

Light concerning Esau's strange action in the selling of his birthright is also found in these Nuzi tablets. A certain man named Tupkitilla in exchange for three sheep transferred his inheritance rights to a grove to his brother Kurpazah. The pertinent portion of the tablet may be rendered as follows:

> On the day that they divide the grove which is on the road of the town of Lumti . . . Tupkitilla shall give it to Kurpazah as his inheritance share (zittu). And Kurpazah has taken three sheep to Tupkitilla in exchange for his inheritance share.

We do not know why Tupkitilla would be willing to part with his birthright for three sheep. In all probability he must have been in dire need. It would seem then, inasmuch as this tablet is an official business document, labeled a tablet of brotherhood, that it was a practice legally recognized and approved that, should a man desire, he might sell his birthright or inheritance rights. The Biblical account of Jacob and Esau is very similar to this Nuzi account of Tupkitilla and Kurpazah.

Of importance is the matter of the relationship between

Jacob and Laban. Here indeed the tablets of Nuzi have shed much light. One of these reads as follows:

> The adoption tablet of Nashwi the son of Arshenni. He adopted Wullu the son of Puhishenni. As long as Nashwi lives, Wullu shall give to him food and clothing. When Nashwi dies, then Wullu shall become the heir. If Nashwi begets a son, he shall divide equally with Wullu but only Nashwi's son shall take Nashwi's gods. If there be no son of Nashwi, then Wullu shall take the gods of Nashwi. And Nashwi has given his daughter Nuhuya as wife to Wullu. And if Wullu takes another wife, he forfeits the land and buildings of Nashwi. Whoever breaks the contract shall pay one mina of silver and one mina of gold.

When Jacob first appears before Laban, there is no evidence that Laban already had sons. Laban agrees to give his daughter to Jacob, and it would seem that Jacob's joining the household of Laban was actually the equivalent of an act of adoption upon the part of Laban. It is of interest to note that in the tablet, the legitimate heir shall receive Nashwi's gods. In the Bible we read of Rachel taking the teraphim and sitting upon them in the tent. (Note that in Gen. 31:30,32 the teraphim are called gods, just as in the Nuzi tablets.) Evidently the possession of these gods implied a position of leadership in the household. By this time Laban had sons of his own and hence we may understand his question, "Why hast thou stolen my gods?" (Gen. 31:30). Laban's indignation, in the light of this tablet, was apparently perfectly justified. On the other hand, Jacob and Rachel were not going to abide by custom. Jacob evidently did not want any secondary position in the household. It would seem that the birth of Laban's sons proved to be a hindrance to Jacob's own desires for himself. If this is the case, and it would seem to be so, we may the more understand the necessity for wrestling with the Lord at Peniel.

Laban did regard Jacob as his adopted son, for he says: "The daughters are my daughters and the children are my children, and the flocks are my flocks, and all that thou seest is mine" (Gen. 31:43, A.S.V.). The plan of Jacob to depart was thus contrary to custom. If Jacob was to be regarded as an adopted son, all that he had was truly Laban's, and in seeking to run away Jacob was violating custom. The Lord, therefore, was gracious in His revelation to Laban: "It is in the power of my hand to do you hurt: but the God of your father spake unto me yesternight, saying, Take heed to thyself that thou speak not to Jacob either good or bad" (Gen. 31:29, A.S.V.; cf. also verse 24).

Laban also violated custom. His daughters made the complaint: "Are we not counted of him strangers [i. e., foreign women]? for he hath sold us, and hath quite devoured also our money" (Gen. 31:15). According to Nuzi there is a sharp distinction to be made between the native women and foreign women. These latter occupied a lower social position, but the native women were not to be subjected to mistreatment. Rachel and Leah evidently believed that Laban had treated them as though they were foreign women.

The patriarchal blessing is also paralleled in the Nuzi tablets. One of the tablets reads, "My father Huya was sick and lying in bed, and my father seized my hand and spoke thus to me: 'My other older sons have taken wives, but thou hast not taken a wife, and I give Zululishtar to thee as a wife.'" This blessing is oral; it is made by a dying father to a son and it also possesses legal validity.

One more point may be noted. Jacob claims, "The rams of thy flocks have I not eaten" (Gen. 31:38). This claim takes on peculiar significance. Apparently the shepherds would very often slaughter lambs and eat mutton at the owner's expense. There are several legal cases concerning this particular matter. Tehiptilla, for example, won at least two cases in law against one of his shepherds who had been killing his sheep clandestinely. Jacob, whatever his faults may have been, at least in this respect was guiltless.

These parallels show conclusively that the background of the patriarchal narratives is one that is in accord with fact. The assertions of those critics who denied the historical character of the patriarchal background have now been shown to be incorrect.

The study of the remarkable tablets from Nuzi is still in its early stages. At the same time enough has already come to light to enable one to say clearly that the background of the patriarchal narratives has been and is being remarkably illumined. These narratives took place against a background which is portrayed in Genesis in a wondrously accurate fashion. Archaeology itself has also made this point clear. The cities mentioned in Genesis were in existence at the time of the patriarchs. The wanderings of the patriarchs took place in the hill country rather than in the coastal plain, and the cities of the hill country have been shown to have been in existence at that time.

b. *Ras Shamra*

One of the most remarkable archaeological discoveries was made in 1929 at Ras Shamra (*Fennelhead*; ancient Ugarit). Of particular interest among the finds are texts written in an alphabetic cuneiform script. While these texts are mythological in nature, they create unusual interest because they are composed in a language very similar to Biblical Hebrew. In several respects they have cast light upon the language of the Bible. For one thing a number of words in the Old Testament, which certain "critics" had designated as late, were found on these texts. Inasmuch as these tablets come from about 1450 b.c., it is clear that the objection which had been raised against the early date of certain Biblical words can no longer be maintained.

As a result of the study of these texts there is manifest upon the part of some "critical" scholars a tendency to date the Psalms earlier than generally has been the case. Little attention is paid in modern criticism to the headings of the Psalms, in respect to the information which they contain regarding the authorship of the particular psalm over which they are placed. In the language of the Ras Shamra texts, however, there is much that is similar to the language of the Psalms. Phrases which occur in the Biblical Psalms also are found in Ras Shamra. It is for this reason, among others, that there is now a tendency to date the Psalms earlier than was previously the case.

Another passage which has received light from Ras Shamra is Isaiah 7:14. It is with respect to the age-old controversy which rages about this verse as to whether the Hebrew word 'almāh is to be translated "young woman" or "virgin." Ras Shamra decides for the latter. One of the texts has to do with the announcement of a wedding among the gods. In announcing the wedding, a formula very similar to Isaiah 7:14 is employed. It is proclaimed, "Behold! a virgin [ǵlmt] will bear a son." On this tablet the word ǵlmt is employed, and just before it, the same announcement had been made, in which the word btlt (virgin) had been used.

The word btlt in Ras Shamra has a more restricted usage than is the case in the Bible. In the Old Testament the Hebrew word may designate a virgin, a betrothed virgin, or even a married woman. In Ras Shamra, however, it is used only in the sense of "virgin," and is often used as a designation of the goddess Anat. As to the word glmt, in Ras Shamra it is always used of an unmarried woman. After the wedding, the woman in question receives a different designation. This fact strengthens the Biblical usage of the word. In the Bible the word 'almāh is never employed of a married woman; the same is true in Ras Shamra, and for that matter in all extra-Biblical literature.

Ras Shamra has thus provided the framework which Isaiah also at a later time employed. As Isaiah used this framework, he, inspired of the Spirit of God, gave to it a richness of content which it had never before received. At the same time, from the formal standpoint, the language of Isaiah and that of Ras Shamra is similar and the latter is actually an aid in enabling one to understand Isaiah.

It now becomes clear that the formula of annunciation which was employed by Isaiah was one which had been widely known in the ancient Near East. For that matter it is also employed elsewhere in the Bible (cf. Gen. 16:11). The usage of this formula makes it clear that there is an unusual birth to be announced. In Ras Shamra it was the birth of a god; in Isaiah it is the birth of the Messiah. In the light of this usage there is no warrant any longer (if there ever has been) for the translation of the word '*almāh* as "young woman."

In the study of the Psalms there have been those who have insisted that the Psalter, and for that matter, other poetry of the Old Testament, must be subjected to an analysis of its metrical structure. It has been claimed that Hebrew poetry contains meter, and upon the basis of this assumption, attempts have been made to scan the Hebrew verses. When the scansion has not proved to be satisfactory, textual emendations have often been proposed.

At this point also the Ugaritic texts have proved to be of great help. These texts are written in poetical form like that of the Old Testament and they also exhibit the phenomenon of parallelism. In respect to the question of meter the Ras Shamra texts have also been studied. It is now known that they present no consistent use of meter. This fact is of the utmost importance, for it makes clear that, just as one is unwarranted in rewriting these mythological poems of Ugarit, so also is he unjustified in rewriting the poetry of the Bible.

There are numerous other points at which Ugaritic is of help in understanding the language of the Old Testament. As far as the grammar and syntax of Hebrew are concerned, these texts are proving to be of inestimable value and benefit. On the whole it may be said that as a result of the discoveries made at Ugarit, a greater respect for the Hebrew text of the Old Testament is being manifested than was formerly the case.

c. *The Dead Sea Scrolls and the Masoretic Text*

The designation Dead Sea Scrolls, refers to certain scrolls, Biblical and non-Biblical, which in recent years have been discovered in caves near the northwestern end of the Dead Sea in Palestine. The initial discovery was made in 1945, and so far some 37 caves have been investigated.

Of particular interest are the discoveries made in the first cave. Of these the most important is the scroll of the Book of Isaiah, containing the entire text. A second manuscript contained the first two chapters of Habakkuk with a commentary. This commentary was distinctive in that it interpreted the text of Habakkuk as referring to events which were contemporary with the commentator himself. A third document had been severed in two. At first it was thought that there were two separate manuscripts, but it was soon seen that the two belonged together. This work came to receive the designation "Manual of Discipline," for it was a code of rules for members of a community. In 1951 ff. the ruins of Khirbet el-Qumran were excavated, and it was this site of Qumran which the community referred to in the Manual at one time inhabited.

Each of these first three documents was written in Hebrew. Unlike them, the fourth was composed in Aramaic. At first it was thought that this fourth scroll was a copy of the lost apocryphal book of Lamech, but when in 1956 the work was finally unrolled, it was declared to be an Aramaic paraphrase of Genesis 5-15 in which some of the characters in Genesis speak in the first person.

The above-mentioned scrolls found their way into the hands of the Syrian monastery of St. Mark in Jerusalem. Three other scrolls also were discovered in the first cave and came into the hands of the late Prof. E. A. Sukenik of the Hebrew University in Jerusalem. Among these three there was also a copy of Isaiah. From chapter 41 to the end the text is reasonably complete, but before chapter 41 it is fragmentary. Another scroll was designated by Sukenik "The War of the Children of Light with the Children of Darkness." It deals with a "holy" war between the Jews (the children of Light who are descendants of Levi, Judah, and Benjamin) and their enemies, "the troops of Edom and Moab, and the children of Ammon, Philistia, and the troops of the Kittim of Asshur." The other manuscript was a collection of hymns of thanksgiving.

As a result of later systematic excavation, a few fragments of papyrus and several hundred of leather were discovered, together with many broken potsherds. Among Biblical fragments there were portions of Genesis, Exodus, Leviticus (probably the oldest of any of the finds in Cave 1), Deuteronomy (written in the old "Phoenician" script), Judges, Samuel, Isaiah, Ezekiel, and the Psalms, and three fragments of Daniel.

In Cave 2, one of the largest near Qumran, further Biblical fragments were found, among which may be mentioned one of Leviticus in early Hebrew script. What was of particular interest in Cave 3 was the discovery in 1952 of two rolled up copper scrolls. In 1956 they were cut into tiny strips, and read. They are said to contain directions for finding treasure. In this cave also one small fragment of what appears to be a commentary on Isaiah was found.

In August, 1952, the Arabs found manuscripts in still another cave (Cave 4). Thousands of fragments were discovered, which had once constituted 330 individual books. Among these every book of the Old Testament except Esther was represented. There were also fragments of non-Biblical books. Of interest are parts of a commentary on Nahum and the Psalms as well as a fragment of Samuel which supports the Septuagint as over against the Masoretic text. In this cave also a fragment of Jeremiah was discovered, which has been dated as coming from about 200 B.C. In Cave 5 fragments in Hebrew and Aramaic of the book of Tobit were discovered, and in Cave 6 a part of the Zadokite work.

In the spring of 1955 more caves were explored, and these have been numbered from 7 to 10. The results were meager, for the material had been largely washed out into the wady (river-bed) itself. In 1956 another cave (No. 11) had been visited by Arabs who found scroll fragments (Leviticus, Psalms ?).

South of Qumran (about twelve miles) at Wady el-Muraba'at more discoveries were made. Fragments of Genesis, Exodus, Deuteronomy, and Isaiah were brought to light, as well as phylacteries. The texts clearly agree with the Masoretic text of the Old Testament.

From Muraba'at there also comes a papyrus in archaic Hebrew characters over which a list of Hebrew names is written (palimpsest). The writing is very old. A number of fragments of Greek papyri were also discovered, and a very brief document in Latin.

Hebrew documents from A.D. 132-135 which mention Simeon ben Kosiba (leader of a revolt against Hadrian) have also come to light. Two letters from Simeon ben Kosiba have been discovered, one of which may mention Christians.

Further Biblical fragments were also discovered in three caves, the precise location of which is not known, and these include Genesis, Numbers, Psalms, a phylactery and a scroll with the Greek text of the Minor Prophets. In Khirbet Mird, west and slightly south of Qumran, a number of Greek and Arabic documents were brought to light (1952), and also some fragments in Syriac. Among the Greek documents mention may be made of Mark, John, and Acts, dating from the fifth to the eighth century A.D. In a later expedition (1953) more fragments were found, including a passage from the *Andromache* of Euripides.

Generally speaking we may place the date of the Qumran manuscripts at about the time of Christ. The earliest are fragments of Samuel and Jeremiah from Cave 4 (*c.* 200 B.C.). The great Isaiah scroll from Cave 1 is probably to be dated about 100 B.C. or earlier. The Habakkuk Commentary, on the other hand, is later and should probably be dated before 63 B.C.

These remarkable manuscript discoveries are proving of greater and greater significance for Biblical studies. And they appear to be bearing out positions which Dr. Wilson espoused.

It is perhaps in order to say a word about the recently discovered manuscripts from the Dead Sea and their relation to the question of the integrity and trustworthiness of the Hebrew text of the Old Testament. At the outset of this discussion, however, a word of caution must be injected. The study of these texts is yet in its infancy. It is still too early to make many dogmatic statements.

Perhaps the most significant of the manuscript finds has been that of the large Book of Isaiah. It is a complete copy of the book, which on the whole is in excellent condition. For the most part it may be said faithfully to represent the Masoretic text, although there are some minor divergencies.

Some fragments which have been discovered support the Septuagint as over against the Masoretic text and some support the Samaritan. What is the reason for this fact?

In all probability Qumran was the site of an ancient religious settlement. Whether the group which dwelt in the monastery were Essenes or not is a difficult question to answer. At least, it would seem, a Jewish group did dwell there. One thing that stands out about this group was its interest in the copying of manuscripts. The remains of a scriptorium have been found, and even a bottle of dried ink. The manuscripts which have been discovered in the caves near Qumran in all probability were copied out in the scriptorium of the monastery. Now, if this was a Jewish sect, and there is little doubt on that point, it is clear that they were not adherents of strict Judaism. They may, therefore, have held to a looser view of the Scriptures, and may have been willing to make minor alterations in the text of Scripture.

Near Qumran is the Wady el-Muraba'at where manuscripts have also been discovered. The manuscripts which have come from this latter place, however, exhibit a remarkable agreement with the Masoretic text. At Wady el-Muraba'at the Jews were those who were in line with the Judaism of the city. Upon the basis of the above facts it would seem that those who were in the strict line of Judaism held also a strict view of the text of Scripture. They would not make emendations in the text even though the emendations might be of a minor nature.

On the other hand, those who had deviated somewhat from strict Judaism were apparently willing to make minor variations in the text. Thus, it is well known that the Samaritans did make such variations in the text of the Pentateuch. It is also well known that the Alexandrian Jews did the same thing. The Septuagint is probably not the first translation of the Old Testament into Greek. It would seem that there had been previous translation. The Alexandrian Jews, being under the influence of Grecian philosophy, were willing to make slight modifications in the text.

If such is the case, we can well understand that the Jews of Qumran, not being in the line of strict Judaism, would in some instances have followed the text types which are illustrated or represented by the Samaritan text and the Greek Septuagint. On the other hand, the Jews of Wady el-Muraba'at, being strict adherents of Judaism, would not deviate from the standard text.

In some such way it would seem, we may explain the presence of minor variations in the Qumran texts. From the beginning, the true followers of the Law possessed a text with which they would not tamper. It is that text which has been handed down to us and which we now designate as Masoretic. On the other hand, expanded texts also began to make their appearance. These texts, for one reason or another, appeared among groups that were not in the main stream of Judaism.

The above analysis must be regarded as merely tentative. On the whole, however, the findings from Qumran may be expected to support the position that the Masoretic text of the Hebrew Old Testament is true and reliable, and this was the very position for which Dr. Wilson so ably contended.

d. *The Alphabet*

Perhaps the first to make use of the alphabetic principle were the Egyptians. Their writing probably arose in the fourth millennium B.C. and it may be that both the idea and method of writing were borrowed by them from the Sumerians. It is probably more accurate to speak of an Egyptian pseudoalphabet than of a genuine alphabet, for the Egyptians did not fully appreciate or make use of the alphabetic principle. They were able to represent consonants without vowels, but not the vowels without consonants.

A fully developed alphabet does appear in Canaan, and it would seem that this alphabet was influenced by Egyptian pictograph writing. In 1904-05 Sir W. M. Flinders Petrie discovered inscriptions at Serabit el-Khadem in the Sinai Peninsula which were in an alphabetic script and provided the connecting link between Egypt and Phoenicia. These inscriptions are to be dated in the early fifteenth century B.C.

Between these Proto-Sinaitic inscriptions and the Phoenician alphabet there is also a link, and this link comes from Palestine itself. The material for study, however, is at present quite meager. From the period between 1800-1500 B.C. there is a potsherd, discovered at Gezer, which has three letters of the type found on the Proto-Sinaitic inscriptions. A plaque from Shechem and two potsherds from the same place together with a bronze dagger from Lachish also have similar characters, although the forms of some of the letters are older than those of the Sinai inscriptions.

From the thirteenth century B.C. there are two inscriptions from Lachish and a jar handle from Tell el-'Ajjûl (in the Negeb). We may note also an inscription from Beth Shemesh and a potsherd from Tell eṣ-Sârem, these latter two dating from about 1200 B.C. or a bit later. This brings us to some javelin heads, which were found by an inhabitant of El-Khaḍr (they were bought from an antiquities dealer in 1953), a village just a short distance west of Bethlehem, which probably date from about 1200 B.C. (the period of the Judges) and provide the connecting link between the Proto-Canaanite inscriptions and the early Phoenician inscriptions (e.g., that of Ahiram *c.* 1000 B.C.).

It is of interest also to note that at Ugarit an alphabet of twenty-nine letters (*c.* 1450 B.C.) was developed. From this brief survey it appears that the alphabet found its origin under Egyptian influence, and that it arose from a script wherein a pictograph stood for the initial sound in the name of the object which the picture represented (the acrophonic principle). This development of the alphabet took place in Syria and Palestine. The Greeks, as is well known, received their alphabet from the Phoenicians.

e. Modern Trends in Old Testament Criticism

The view of the Old Testament which was regnant during Dr. Wilson's day among those who denied the infallibility of Scripture has suffered such serious setbacks that it can no longer be regarded as dominant. For one thing the inherent weaknesses of the Wellhausen reconstruction of Israel's history began more and more to be recognized. The discoveries of archaeology also caused a shift from Wellhausen's views and made it clear that these latter were not always founded on fact.

As a result of archaeological investigation, there has appeared a tendency to attribute greater historical value to the Old Testament. William F. Albright has been a leader in the study of archaeology in relation to the Old Testament. Scandinavian scholars have laid greater stress on oral tradition and on the study of the Old Testament against its environment. All of this has caused a modification of that aspect of Wellhausen's views known as the Development Hypothesis (i.e., the view that the institutions and religion of Israel underwent a certain development, contrary to the picture given by the Old Testament itself).

On the other hand, the Documentary Hypothesis (i.e., the view that the Pentateuch consists of different documents, commonly labeled J, E, D, and P) is still quite widely held. Its principal modification is in the appearance of a view that the first four books of the Bible constitute a Tetrateuch and represent a certain complex of tradition. Side by side with this Tetrateuch there is said to exist the Deuteronomic

Work, which represented another body of tradition. Archaeology does not appear to have affected seriously belief in the Documentary Theory. One can only hope that more careful study of the contents of the Biblical books will reveal the inherent weaknesses of the Documentary Theory.

GLOSSARY

To make this work of greater help to the average reader not acquainted with the technical terms of Biblical criticism and philology, this glossary has been prepared in explanation of some of the more important of these terms.

ACHAEMENID. Achaemenes was the great-grandfather of Darius the Great, king of Persia in the days of Marathon, 522 to 486 B.C. The Persian kings of this dynasty are called Achaemenids

ASHURBANIPAL. Ashurbanipal was the last great king of Assyria and reigned from 666 to 626 B.C. The best work on him is in three volumes by Streck.

BAR HEBRAEUS. Bar-Hebraeus, or Abu'l-Faraj Gregory, was a Jewish convert to Christianity and "one of the most learned and versatile men that Syria ever produced." (See Wright: *Syriac Literature,* 265-281.) The account of the conquest of Jerusalem will be found in the *Chronicon Syriacum* (263-266), sold by Maissoneuve, Paris.

BEHISTUN. Behistun, the ancient Bagistana, is the name of a village on the highway between Babylonia and Ecbatana (Hamadan), the capital of Media. On the face of a rock 500 feet above the plain are inscriptions of Darius the Great in Persian, Elamitic, and Babylonian. (See Eduard Meyer in *Encyclopedia Britannica,* III, 656; Weissbach and Bang: *Die altpersischen Keilinschriften,* 1893; King and Thompson: *The Inscription of Darius the Great at Behistun,* 1907; and works by Prof. A. V. Williams Jackson.) An Aramaic recension of this inscription was found in Egypt and published by Edouard Sachau in his *Aramäische Papyrus und Ostraka,* 1911. [Reviewed by the writer in the PTR for 1914.] It is to be found also in Cowley's *Aramaic Papyri of the Fifth Century* B.C.

BEN SIRA. Name of the writer of the apocryphal book of Ecclesiasticus.

CARTOUCHES. A cartouche is an oval or oblong figure in an Egyptian document, containing the name of a sovereign.

CONSONANTAL TEXT. Only the consonants and, in some cases, the vowel letters *w* to denote ô and û and *y* to denote ê and î, were used in the Old Testament text before about A.D. 600, at which time vowel signs were added.

DEAD SEA SCROLLS. (See Appendix 2C.) A reliable introduction to the study of these scrolls will be found in F. F. Bruce: *Second Thoughts on the Dead Sea Scrolls,* 1956.

DIM. Sumerian word for create and make. (See Delitzsch: *Sumerisches Glossar,* p. 138.)

ELEPHANTINE. Elephantine was the name of a city on an island at the first cataract of the Nile. Its name denotes elephant in the Egyptian abu, as well as in the Greek from which the English is merely a transliteration. Opposite the island was the city of Syene or Assouan. It is about 551 miles by rail from Cairo.

GLOSS. An explanatory word or phrase. In the Amarna Letters the Hebrew glosses explain the Babylonian words.

GRIMM'S LAW. *Grimm's law* is the name for the regular interchange of certain consonants in the so-called Indo-European family of languages. See Max Müller's *Lectures on the Science of Language,* II. Lecture V; Skeat's *Principles of English Etymology,* p. 104; and Whitney's *Language and the Study of Language.*

HAMMURABI. Hammurabi (or pi) "the mighty king, the king of Babylon, the king of the four quarters," as he calls himself (see King: *The Letters and Inscriptions of Hammurabi,* p. 179), seems at first to have been subject to Elam, whose king he overthrew in his thirty-first year *(idem* 23).

HAPAX LEGOMENA. Words occurring only in a document.

HEXATEUCH. First six books of the Bible. Writers on the first six books of the Old Testament commonly employ the letters H, P, J, E, D, to denote the five sources of these books as claimed by the critics.

> P denotes the so-called priest-codex, which is supposed to have been written after the time of Ezekiel. Broadly, it embraces all of Leviticus, except chapters 17-26, nearly all of Numbers, a large part especially of the latter part of Exodus, parts of Genesis (especially the first chapter), and about a third of Joshua.

H is named from holiness *(Heiligkeit)* and gets its name from the fact that it emphasizes the laws of holiness. It is found in Leviticus 17-26. It is supposed to have been written during the captivity.

D stands for Deuteronomy, and embraces most of Deuteronomy and about a third of Joshua.

J comes from the word Jehovah, and embraces a large part of Genesis and Exodus 1-19, characterized by having the name Jehovah in it.

E comes from Elohim, the Hebrew name for God, and includes the parts of the Hexateuch which contain the name Elohim for God and which do not belong to P.

JE stands for the parts in which J and E cannot be distinguished.

HIPHIL. Name of a Hebrew verbal form which usually has a causative sense.

JONATHAN. Name given the version of the pseudonymous author of a second Aramaic version of the books of Moses.

JOSHUA THE STYLITE. Joshua the Stylite was a Monophysite Stylite monk who lived at Edessa in the early part of the sixth century and wrote a history of the war between the Byzantine and Persian empires which took place from A.D. 502 to 506. See Wright's *Syriac Literature,* pp. 77, 78, and his work called *The Chronicle of Joshua the Stylite.*

LACHISH LETTERS. These documents were discovered in 1935 in the excavations of Tell ed-Duweir in Palestine. They are letters, belonging to the time of the destruction of Jerusalem and are of great interest for the light which they shed on that period.

MANTIS. A sort of prophet-priest of the Greeks.

MARI. Name of an ancient city of the Euphrates River in Mesopotamia. The modern site is known as Tell el Hariri. Excavations were begun here in 1935, with the result that some 20,000 tablets have been unearthed. These tablets support the Biblical viewpoint that Israel's ancestors came from Harran. The texts are proving extremely interesting for the light which they shed on the background of the time *(c.* 1850 B.C.).

MASORETES. Jewish scribes and learned men who edited the text of the Old Testament Scriptures.

MESHA INSCRIPTION. The Mesha inscription, also called the Moabite stone, contains an inscription by Mesha, King of

Moab, and was found by a missionary named Klein among the ruins of the city of Dibon in the land of Moab in the year 1868. It has been treated in monographs by Smend, Clermont-Ganneau, Nöldeke, Nordlander, and others. The text will be found in Lidzbarski's *Nordsemitische Epigraphik*.

MOABITE STONE. See Mesha Inscription above.

MORPHOLOGY. The science of the forms of words.

NABUNAID (OR NABONIDUS). Name of the last *de facto* and *de jure* king of Babylon according to the monuments; Belshazzar according to the Scriptures being the last *de facto* king.

NUZI. Name of an ancient site in Mesopotamia, known now as Yorgan Tepe. The place was a center of Hurrian civilization. Tablets found at this site are significant for the study of the Patriarchal Period. (See Appendix 2a.)

ONKELOS. Name of the author of the best Aramaic version of the books of Moses. The version is named after him.

OSTRAKA. Fragments of pottery on which are Hebrew, Greek, or Coptic inscriptions.

PALEOGRAPHY. Ancient ways of indicating words in writing, and the study or art of deciphering them.

PESHITTO. See Versions.

POINTINGS. Signs added to the original consonantal text in order to indicate the sound or the sense of the original according to the view of the exegete or pointer.

PREFORMATIVES AND SUFFORMATIVES. Semitic roots have commonly three consonantal letters. Many nouns and forms of the verb are formed from these roots by putting a consonant before or after. When placed before, the consonant is called a preformative; when after, a sufformative.

PROSTHETIC. A letter, commonly Aleph, prefixed to another with *e* or *a* to aid in the pronunciation. Thus in Ashtora for Shtora and in Ahasuerus the *A* is prosthetic.

PROTASIS. The clause introduced by "if," "when," "whoever," etc., upon which the main proposition depends. Thus "if you love me" is the protasis of which "ye will keep my commandments" is the apodosis.

PROVENANCE. The locality at which any antique is found or document was written.

PSEUDEPIGRAPH. A writing ascribed to one who did not write it. In works on the canon it is commonly restricted to documents which are not in the canon of the Roman Catholics. Apocryphal are the books acknowledged by the Roman Catholics, but not by Protestants.

PYRAMID TEXTS. *Die Pyramidentexte* is the name given to a series of Egyptian inscriptions found in the pyramids. They have been published in the "*Recueil de travaux relatifs à la philologie et à l' archéologie égyptienne et assyrienne.*" The first of these texts were those found in the pyramid of King Ounas the last king of the fifth dynasty. They were edited by Maspéro and published in 1882.

RADICAL SOUNDS. The three consonants used in a root are called radicals.

RAS SHAMRA (Fennelhead). The modern designation of the ancient city of Ugarit. It is located near the Syrian coast, north of Beirut. The discoveries were made in 1929, and the alphabetic cuneiform texts date from about 1450 B.C.

RECENSION. A text established by revision and editing, either by the author or by another. Thus, there is a longer recension of Jeremiah preserved in the Hebrew Bible and a shorter in the Greek; and there are two recensions of the Ten Commandments, one in Exodus 20 and one in Deuteronomy 5. So, there are at least two recensions of the inscription of Darius at Behistun, the longer being that contained in the Persian, of which the Elamite is apparently a translation, and the shorter in the Babylonian which is fairly equivalent to the Aramaic. The first three are certainly and the Aramaic probably from the same time and have the same authority. Sometimes we speak of the whole four as recensions.

REDACTORS. Editors who put together and supplemented the original parts of the Pentateuch.

SACHAU PAPYRI. The Sachau Papyri (or Papyrus) are Aramaic documents (mostly letters and contracts, but containing also a short edition of the Behistun inscription of Darius the Great, king of Persia, and part of a story of a man called Achikar) edited by Prof. Edouard Sachau of the University of Berlin. (See my review in the PTR for 1911.)

SAMARITAN. Here used for the version of the books of Moses into the Samaritan dialect of the Aramaic. This version is still used by a small number of persons residing in the modern city of Nablous.

SAMARITAN VERSION. See Versions.

SENDSCHIRLI INSCRIPTIONS. Six inscriptions in the Sendschirli dialect are published in Lidzbarski's *Nordsemitische Epigraphik.* The first of these, embracing 34 lines, is by Panammu, king of Jadi and Sam'al, and the second, third and fourth by his son Barrekeb. The others are small fragments.

SEPTUAGINT. The translation of the Old Testament into Greek, about 250-150 B.C.

SILOAM INSCRIPTION. The Siloam inscription in Hebrew was found in 1880 on a wall of the conduit built by Hezekiah (Isa. 22:11). It is the oldest inscription of any length in the Hebrew language. See Lidzbarski: *Nordsemitische Inschriften.*

SUMERIAN. Name of the people who preceded the Semites in Babylon and apparently invented the system of writing afterward used by the Assyrians, Babylonians, Hittites and others.

SURAS. Name for the chapters of the Koran.

SYRIAC. The name given to the dialect of Aramaic spoken in Mesopotamia at Edessa. The common version is called the Syriac Peshitto, and is cited either as Peshitto, or Syriac.

TARGUM. There is only one targum, or translation, to the prophets in Aramaic, called the targum of Jonathan Ben Uzziel. See Stenning in *Encyclopedia Britannica* XXVI, 421. See also Versions.

TEL-EL-AMARNA LETTERS. The Tel-el-Amarna or El-Amarna Letters were discovered in 1888 at Tel-el-Amarna in Egypt and date from the reigns of Amenhotep III and IV. They were written in cuneiform, mostly in the Babylonian language, from Babylon, Assyria, Syria, Palestine, and other countries, to the kings of Egypt, and some of them from the kings of Egypt in reply.

TETRATEUCH. *Teuch* is from a word which in post-Alexandrine Greek means "book." *Penta* means "five," *hexa* "six," and *tetra* "four." It is used on page 52 for the books from Exodus to Deuteronomy inclusive.

TEXTUS RECEPTUS. The "received text"; the text published in our ordinary Hebrew Bibles.

TIDAL. Tidal, king of nations (Gen. 14:1). If the Hebrew *goyim*, "nations," is a rendering of *kiššati*, it is found as a title of Shalmanassar I of Assyria about 1300 B.C. and of Ramman-Nirari his father and was probably used of his ancestors back as far at least as Asuruballit. See Schrader in The Cuneiform Library (KAT I. 9). It is used at Babylon also, of Merodach-Baladan I about 1200 B.C. *(idem* III¹ 162).

If we assume that the Hebrew text comes from Kutim, the phrase "king of Kutim" is found as early as Naram-Sin, long before Hammurabi and Abraham. (See Thureau-Dangin: *Sumerische und Akkadische Königinschriften*, p. 225) where we read that Sharlak, king of the Kuti, was taken by Sargani-shar-ali, and (p. 226) where something was done to the land of the Kuti. See also p. 171, where a tablet of Lasirab king of Gutim is given.)

TRANSLATE. To render the sense or meaning of one language into another language.

TRANSLITERATE. To give the letters of the original, as in *Alleluia.*

UGARIT. Ancient name of the site which today is known as Ras Shamra.

VERSIONS. There are three versions of the books of Moses from the Hebrew language in which they were originally written into the Aramaic which many of the Israelites learned and spoke from some time before the time of Christ and for many centuries after. Targum is the Aramaic word for version.

Latin Vulgate. The Latin Vulgate is the translation made by Jerome from Hebrew into Latin about A.D. 400. It is the Bible used today by the Roman Catholic church. See Kaulen: *Geschichte der Vulgata*, and Berger: *La Bible Francaise au Moyen-age.*

Samaritan Version. The Samaritan version is the translation of the Samaritan Hebrew recension of the books of Moses. It is still used by the small Samaritan synagogue in Nablous in Palestine.

Syriac Peshitto. The Syriac Peshitto is the name of the version commonly used in the Syrian churches. Peshitto means simple or explained.

VOWEL SIGNS. See Consonantal text.

VOCABLE. A word, or vocal sound.

VULGATE. See Versions.

WAU CONJUNCTIVE. The Hebrew conjunction *w*, meaning "and."

WAU CONVERSIVE. The Hebrew conjunction *w* "and" when used before the perfect, or imperfect form of the verb, with the power of converting the perfect into the sense of the imperfect or the imperfect into the sense of the perfect.

ZADOKITE FRAGMENTS. The Zadokite Fragments are the portions of a work in Hebrew supposed to have been written about the time of Christ. See Charles: *Apocrypha and Pseudepigrapha of the Old Testament,* II. 785-854, Schechter's *Documents of Jewish Sectaries,* and Chaim Rabin, *The Zadokite Fragments,* Oxford, 1954. (Contains the text with a translation and notes.)

INDEX

OTHER RELATED SOLID GROUND TITLES

The Origin of Paul's Religion by J. Gresham Machen was the first book written by one of the leading apologists of the early 20th century.

Notes on Galatians by J. Gresham Machen is a reprint that is long overdue, especially in light of the present-day battle of the doctrine articulated in Galatians.

Opening Scripture: A Hermeneutical Manual by Patrick Fairbairn is a favorite volume of Sinclair Ferguson. Once again you will find help in these long-buried pages to combat many errors in today's church.

Biblical and Theological Studies by the professors of Princeton Seminary in 1912, at the centenary celebration of the Seminary. Articles are by men like Allis, Vos, Warfield, Machen, Wilson and others.

Theology on Fire: Vols. 1 & 2 by Joseph A. Alexander is the two volumes of sermons by this brilliant scholar from Princeton Seminary.

A Shepherd's Heart by James W. Alexander is a volume of outstanding expository sermons from the pastoral ministry of one of the leading preachers of the 19th century.

Evangelical Truth by Archibald Alexander is a volume of practical sermons intended to be used for Family Worship.

The Lord of Glory by Benjamin B. Warfield is one of the best treatments of the doctrine of the Deity of Christ ever written. Warfield is simply masterful.

The Power of God unto Salvation by Benjamin B. Warfield is the first book of sermons ever published of this master-theologian. Several of these are found no where else.

Mourning a Beloved Shepherd by Charles Hodge and John Hall is a little volume containing the funeral addresses for James W. Alexander. Very informative and challenging.

Call us Toll Free at 1-877-666-9469
Send us an e-mail at sgcb@charter.net
Visit us on line at solid-ground-books.com